JESSE OWENS

Recent Titles in Greenwood Biographies

JESSE OWENS

A Biography

Jacqueline Edmondson

GREENWOOD BIOGRAPHIES

GREENWOOD PRESS
WESTPORT, CONNECTICUT • LONDON

Library of Congress Cataloging-in-Publication Data

Edmondson, Jacqueline.
  Jesse Owens: a biography / by Jacqueline Edmondson.
    p. cm. — (Greenwood Biographies, ISSN 1540–4900)
  Includes bibliographical references and index.
  ISBN 978–0–313–33988–2 (alk. paper)
    1. Owens, Jesse, 1913–1980.   2. Track and field athletes—United States—Biography.
I. Title.
GV697.O9E35 2007
796.42092—dc22   2007021680
[B]

British Library Cataloguing in Publication Data is available.

Library of Congress Catalog Card Number: 2007021680
ISBN-13: 978–0–313–33988–2
ISSN: 1540–4900

First published in 2007

Greenwood Press, 88 Post Road West, Westport, CT 06881
An imprint of Greenwood Publishing Group, Inc.
www.greenwood.com

Printed in the United States of America

The paper used in this book complies with the
Permanent Paper Standard issued by the National
Information Standards Organization (Z39.48–1984).

10 9 8 7 6 5 4 3 2 1

To my sons Jacob and Luke
To my nephews Asher and Connor

CONTENTS

Photo essay follows page 36.

SERIES FOREWORD

In response to high school and public library needs, Greenwood developed this distinguished series of full-length biographies specifically for student use. Prepared by field experts and professionals, these engaging biographies are tailored for high school students who need challenging yet accessible biographies. Ideal for secondary school assignments, the length, format and subject areas are designed to meet educators' requirements and students' interests.

Greenwood offers an extensive selection of biographies spanning all curriculum related subject areas including social studies, the sciences, literature and the arts, history and politics, as well as popular culture, covering public figures and famous personalities from all time periods and backgrounds, both historic and contemporary, who have made an impact on American and/or world culture. Greenwood biographies were chosen based on comprehensive feedback from librarians and educators. Consideration was given to both curriculum relevance and inherent interest. The result is an intriguing mix of the well known and the unexpected, the saints and sinners from long-ago history and contemporary pop culture. Readers will find a wide array of subject choices from fascinating crime figures like Al Capone to inspiring pioneers like Margaret Mead, from the greatest minds of our time like Stephen Hawking to the most amazing success stories of our day like J.K. Rowling.

While the emphasis is on fact, not glorification, the books are meant to be fun to read. Each volume provides in-depth information about the subject's life from birth through childhood, the teen years, and adult-hood. A thorough account relates family background and education, traces personal and professional influences, and explores struggles, ac-complishments, and contributions. A timeline highlights the most significant life events against a historical perspective. Bibliographies supplement the reference value of each volume.

ACKNOWLEDGMENTS

I want to offer a special word of appreciation to Marlene Owens Rankin, Jesse Owens's youngest daughter. She was always very responsive to my questions as I worked through the research for this book. I am most appreciative of the time she took to review the manuscript to ensure that the facts of her father's life were accurate.

I want to thank Robert Pruter of the Lewis University Library for help he provided to me in finding historical information about track and field events. I also want to give credit to The Ohio State University Archives for answering questions about track and field at the university when Jesse Owens was there.

Dr. Murry Nelson was a continual source of support, conversation, and information as I worked through this project. He was kind enough to read an earlier draft of this book to be sure I had accurate historical information. I also want to thank Alexandra D'Urso, my research assistant, for her careful reading and editing of this manuscript.

Finally, I want to thank my husband Michael for the patient support he always provides when I am writing, and for his willingness to listen and read as I work through drafts of chapters. I also want to thank my sons Jacob and Luke, who help me to understand the perspectives and questions young people bring to biographies.

INTRODUCTION

It speaks to my dad's philosophy that we are all one race—the human race—and if we all work together what a wonderful, wonderful place this would be.

—Gloria Owens Hemphill, as quoted in Pacey 1996

On a hot June day in 1996, Stuart Owen Rankin, a young African American, ran into the Jesse Owens Memorial Park in Oakville, Alabama, with an Olympic torch in his hand. Rankin was one of 10,000 torchbearers who would pass the flame from one runner to the next until it reached its final destination at the Atlanta summer games. Rankin's selection as a torchbearer and his run through Oakville in Lawrence County was significant. Rankin was the grandson of Olympic hero Jesse Owens, and he was passing through the community where Owens, as a young boy, had first run across fields and dusty country roads to feel some measure of freedom in the midst of the racial problems of the Deep South. A sharecropper's son, Owens was born when the world was on the brink of World War I, and attained Olympic glory with the world on the brink of World War II. Owens spent his early years struggling to overcome poverty and illness, and he grew up to run faster and jump further than anyone could have imagined.

Many communities readily embrace their heroes, but Lawrence County struggled for more than 50 years to come to terms with Jesse Owens and his legacy. Even though Owens made world history at the 1936 Olympic

Games, winning four gold medals for his track performance on the mud-covered fields of the Berlin Olympic Stadium and setting records that would stand in some cases for two decades, the town council and citizens were reluctant to publicly acknowledge the accomplishments of this well-known African American. In 1983, the all-white county commission unanimously rejected plans to build a statue for the Olympic hero in front of the county courthouse (Johnson 1995). When word of this vote reached the public, a small group of African American Masons cleared a patch of land on the edge of town and erected a small memorial to the track legend. The memorial was modest, consisting of a concrete basketball court, a small marker with an incorrect birth date, and a display case with faded photographs of Owens. Unremarkable as the memorial was, someone still tried to ruin it, attaching a chain to the marker in an effort to pull it out of the ground in the middle of the night (Greenburg 1996).

As young Rankin made his way to the park that commemorated his grandfather's life and victories, he ran past racist signs painted on a bridge and through an area beset by racial tensions that in some ways seemed to be little changed from the time his grandfather was a child. A crowd of onlookers cheered as Rankin passed them. Among them were his grandmother Ruth, his mother Marlene, and his aunts Gloria and Beverly. Although none had been to Lawrence County before, this connection to Owens's past was significant for each. The celebratory day was proclaimed as Jesse Owens Day, but all knew that this victory had not been easily earned. Yet, the memorial park indicated some measure of success in easing racial tensions in the community. African Americans and whites from the community came together to work on the park, and many admitted to having a better understanding of one another as a result. To acknowledge this, Rankin passed the torch on to two men, one white and one African American, who symbolically carried the torch out of the park together.

Understanding Jesse Owens requires that we appreciate his own complicated experiences as they unfolded across the twentieth century. For young people today, it may be difficult to imagine a time when African Americans were not part of professional sports in the United States. So many admired and beloved African American athletes are heroes to young people today: Michael Jordan, Venus and Serena Williams, Tiger Woods, Florence Griffith Joyner, Shaquille O'Neal, and Muhammad Ali, to name a few. These athletes have a prominent place in American culture and the hearts of American people. But there were no such celebrity athletes when Owens was a boy, and no African American stars for him to hope to emulate. There was no one the young boy could set his sights on and say, "I want to be like that some day." Instead, his athletic accomplishments were achieved against many seemingly insurmountable odds, including his own imagination. How could he ever have dreamed, when he ran through the fields of Oakville as a poor, hungry, and frequently ill child, that he would one day win races as the world watched?

As Owens began to break world records in track and gain attention from the general public, there were few other athletes who could understand his experiences, including the overt racial discrimination he faced, and there were even fewer who understood the complexities his fame brought. One exception was Owens's friend, boxer Joe Louis. Louis was born eight months after Owens in LaFayette, Alabama. Like Owens, his father was a sharecropper and his grandfather was a slave. Both moved north with their families in the 1920s, and both found a future in sports. Owens and Louis paved the way for other black athletes, including Jackie Robinson, who is credited with breaking the color barrier in professional sports. Joe Louis's son explained to writer Donald McRae, "Jesse and my father were pioneers. They changed and challenged America's conscience. Out of the terrible adversity and suffering of Jesse and Joe came real beauty and courage. And at least they were not alone. They had each other. They were great friends" (2002, 7). Owens later wrote that he and Louis were closer than brothers could be "because it was as if we'd been the only two of our kind for a long, long time. It would've been lonesome as hell without knowing there was at least one other" (1972, 72). Louis and Owens died within a year of each other, each at age 66.

Owens experienced racism and poverty during a time that seems somewhat far removed from our present circumstances, and this can make it more challenging to fully grasp what he faced. Owens was the first in his family to attend college, and he earned fame and money beyond anyone's expectation. Yet along with this fame came loss and struggle. No one would claim that Owens had an easy life either before or after he won Olympic gold. While Owens may have brought some of his struggles upon himself through poor business decisions or other lapses in judgment, other problems he faced were part of larger, systemic issues in the United States. Owens knew what it meant to face racial discrimination and to be excluded based only on the color of his skin. There were times when he was not offered jobs because of his race, and times when he could not eat in a restaurant because it served whites only. There are no easy or straightforward explanations to the challenges Owens encountered during his lifetime. Yet we must carefully consider these problems, learn from them, and work to bring changes to the issues that remain in our society today.

Owens was well loved by many, yet like any famous person, he had critics. Most notably, people judged him for appearing not to stand up to white people and for not being more critical of Jim Crow laws and the inequitable treatment he suffered because of his race. In the face of this criticism Owens was not willing to concede that his views were wrong. While he appreciated the causes that Martin Luther King, Jr. and other prominent activists fought for, he was not willing to engage these debates in the same way. While he deeply admired King, Owens was opposed to the nonviolence that King endorsed, explaining instead "if a man hits you, sometimes you must hit back" (Owens 1970, 89). At the same time, Owens would not support the militant approach of the Black Panthers and other civil rights groups. Instead, he hoped to change the world by living in it.

As readers of Owens's story, we could analyze his ideas and actions according to our contemporary understandings of racism, or we could attempt instead to understand how Owens experienced racism as a young man who grew up in poverty in the Deep South, won Olympic gold in Hitler's Germany by running faster and jumping farther than anyone in the world, and achieved fame and sometimes fortune in the midst of two World Wars and other times of hardship in the United States. Throughout this book, I attempt to do the latter; that is, I hope to help readers understand Owens's views on race and racism as they were historically and culturally situated. To do this, I rely on his words and accounts of what he experienced and why. I also rely on explanations offered to me from his three daughters—Marlene, Beverly, and Gloria. Understanding this past can give us new insight into the present and help us to imagine different possibilities for the future.

A NOTE ON SOURCES

This book was challenging to write. Jesse Owens is certainly a key figure in American history. Because of his fame and accomplishments, a great deal has been written about him. However, various accounts often contain contradictory or incomplete information. For example, some accounts of Owens's childhood mention that he was the youngest of 10 children in the Owens family, while others state that he was the seventh of 11 children. Some accounts say that he was born in Oakville, Alabama (Owens 1978), while others name Danville, Alabama (FBI 1956). Sometimes exact dates of events are difficult to ascertain. Because of Owens's fame, there are also certain myths that surround his life. In writing this book, I was careful to use reliable sources and to cross-check those sources against others. In addition, I was fortunate to be able to correspond with

Marlene Owens Rankin, Owens's youngest daughter. She was willing to carefully read the manuscript to ensure that the details were correct.

There were a few texts that were key to writing this book and that are worth mentioning at the outset of this biography. Owens wrote several autobiographical pieces with Paul Neimark that were useful, although none are comprehensive stories of the entirety of his life. Instead, the autobiographies are organized in ways that help to tell select stories and teach lessons to the reader. The most comprehensive account of Owens's life is the book *Jesse: The Man Who Outran Hitler* (1978). This was an important resource as I sought to understand Owens's childhood and young adult life. He organized the book around key events so that readers could get a sense of his experiences.

Blackthink: My Life as Black Man and White Man (1970) helped me to understand more about the racism Owens faced, and his hopes for how society could change. This autobiography, which won the Martha Cooper award for best human relations book of the year, was Owens's attempt to create a third, racially neutral position in the United States to unite people differently around issues of race and racism. However, Owens realized that he did not achieve this goal with his book, and he acknowledged that there was no such thing as a third position. Owens felt he needed to try again. The book *I Have Changed* (1972) followed. It began with Owens telling a story about being in a barbershop in Chicago and overhearing his friends speculate about his upcoming move to Phoenix, Arizona. His barbershop buddies joked that Owens was moving west because black people were moving into his Chicago neighborhood. The comment was deeply painful to Owens because he felt the men believed their false explanation to be true. As a result, he attempted to clarify his position through this book.

The book *Track and Field* (1976), written by Owens and edited by Dick O'Connor, gives young people tips on being successful in various track and field events. There are occasional times in the book where Owens writes about his own experiences in track and field, and how these events changed from the time of his youth until the time that he wrote the book.

In addition to these autobiographical accounts, Donald McRae's 2002 book *Heroes without a Country* does a wonderful job expressing the impact that Jesse Owens and Joe Louis had on American sports. The book recounts their lives and experiences, relying on firsthand interviews with family members and friends of both men. Finally, Richard Mandell's book *The Nazi Olympics* (1971) was a key resource to explain the 1936 Olympics and the events leading up to it.

There are some films that were also very instrumental in helping me to understand Jesse Owens, his family, and his accomplishments. *The Jesse Owens Story* was a 1984 made-for-TV movie that starred Dorian Harewood as Jesse Owens. Marlene recommended this to me as one of the best representations of the Owens family. Leni Riefenstahl's work in *Olympia*, the controversial film of the 1936 Olympics Games, gave me an opportunity to see Jesse Owens in his historic runs. The film has wonderful coverage of his races, and nice close-up shots of Owens as a young athlete. Finally, *Jesse Owens Returns to Berlin* offers a reflection on the Olympic experience, and Jesse Owens narrated the entire thing, allowing viewers to hear his voice throughout the film. I recommend these films to any reader who would like to see Jesse Owens run and hear him speak. A complete list of resources used in writing this book is found at the end of the text, and I make reference to sources throughout the book so readers can understand the sources for certain key points.

In closing, I must offer a special note of appreciation to Marlene for her correspondence with me about this project. She was quite concerned that the facts of her father's story are correct, and she was always willing to answer any questions that I had about his life. She also took considerable care reading through the final draft, making notes, and offering suggestions. This project has benefited tremendously from of her contributions.

TIMELINE: SIGNIFICANT EVENTS IN THE LIFE OF JESSE OWENS

1913   James Cleveland "Jesse" Owens is born September 12 in Oakville, Alabama.

1914   On May 13 or 14 (sources differ), Joe Louis Barrow (a.k.a. Joe Louis, or the Brown Bomber) is born in Alabama. The Sixteenth Amendment to the Constitution is passed into law.

1917   The United States enters World War I. Over 15 million lives are lost during the war.

1919   The Weimar Republic is formed in Germany.

1920   The Owens family leaves rural Alabama for a new life in Cleveland, Ohio.

1928   The Olympic Games are held in Amsterdam, and for the first time include women's track and field events.

1931   The International Olympic Committee awards the next game venue to Berlin, Germany.

1932   Owens and Ruth welcome their first child, Gloria, to the family on August 8. The Olympics are held in Los Angeles, California.

1933   Jesse Owens enters The Ohio State University.

1935   Owens breaks three world records and ties a fourth at the Big Ten Championships on May 25. He later called this his best day. On July 23, he meets boxer Joe Louis for the first time. The two become lifelong friends.

1936   Owens wins four gold medals during the Berlin Olympic Games. Owens is named Associated Press Athlete of the Year, just one

year after boxer Joe Louis won the same award. No other
African American athlete earned the award again until
Willie Mays in 1954. The World Labor Athletics Carnival, the
counter-Olympics, is held in New York City to protest the Berlin
games.

1937   On July 7, Japan invades China, beginning the Second
Sino-Japanese War. Ruth and Owens's second child, Beverly, is
born on October 5.

1938   The Jesse Owens Dry Cleaning Company is founded.

1939   Marlene Owens, the Owens' third daughter, is born on
April 19. Germany invades Poland on September 1, and Great
Britain and France declare war on Germany two days later,
marking the beginning of what would become World War II.

1940   Jesse Owens endorses Franklin Delano Roosevelt for a third term
as U.S. president. Emma, Owens's mother, dies. Seven months
later, his father Henry dies.

1941   On December 7, the Japanese attack Pearl Harbor, and the
United States enters World War II. On December 11, Germany
and Italy declare war on the United States. Ruth's father, Gus
Solomon, passes away.

1942   President Roosevelt signs Executive Order 9066 in February,
authorizing the army to arrest every Japanese American on the
West Coast of the U.S. and remove them to internment camps.
Jesse Owens moves to Detroit to work for the Ford Motor
Company as a personnel director.

1945   On April 12, Harry S. Truman becomes the 33rd president of
the United States when FDR dies of a cerebral hemorrhage. On
April 30, Hitler commits suicide as Russian forces take the city
of Berlin. Germany surrenders to Allied forces on May 2. On
August 6, the United States drops an atomic bomb on
Hiroshima. On August 9, the United States drops an atomic
bomb on Nagasaki. The Japanese surrender on August 15.

1947   Jackie Robinson breaks the color barrier in professional baseball.

1948   Mel Patton beats Owens's 1936 record for the 100-yard dash.
Fanny Blankers-Koen of the Netherlands wins four gold medals
in the Olympics in London, the only woman to do so.

1950   Owens is named Greatest Athlete of the Past 50 Years in an
Associated Press poll. On June 25, the Korean War begins.

1951   Owens returns to Berlin and the Olympic stadium with the
Harlem Globetrotters. He meets Karl Long, son of his Olympic
friend and competitor Luz Long.

1953   Dwight D. Eisenhower becomes 34th president of the United
       States. The Korean War ends. Gloria Owens graduates from
       Ohio State with a BS in education.

1954   Owens takes a position as youth director for the Illinois Athletic
       Commission.

1955   As ambassador of sports for the U.S. government, Owens visits
       Bombay, India. He promotes athletics and democracy in
       countries around the world.

1956   Owens serves as President Eisenhower's representative to the
       Olympic Games in Sydney, Australia. J. Edgar Hoover launches
       an investigation of Owens's private life. Owens travels abroad on
       a goodwill tour of India, Malaysia, and the Philippines to
       promote goodwill, democracy, and freedom.

1957   The Soviet Union successfully launches Sputnik. Beverly Owens
       elopes, marrying Donald Prather, a school principal. Gloria
       Owens marries Malcolm Hemphill, a schoolteacher and coach.

1960   Marlene Owens is the first black woman elected Homecoming
       Queen at Ohio State.

1961   John F. Kennedy becomes the 35th president of the United
       States. Marlene Owens marries Stuart M. Rankin, an advertising
       executive.

1963   President Kennedy is assassinated on November 22. Lyndon B.
       Johnson becomes the 36th president of the United States.

1964   U.S. involvement in Vietnam escalates after the Gulf of Tonkin
       incident, where the United States claimed North Korea at-
       tacked two of its destroyers.

1965   Owens is convicted of income tax evasion, with lawyers' fees
       and fines totaling $150,000. A partially ruptured spinal disc
       forces Owens to undergo back surgery.

1966   Eldridge Cleaver is released from prison and joins the Black
       Panther Party.

1968   Martin Luther King Jr. is assassinated in April, and Robert F.
       Kennedy is assassinated in June. Mexican police kill more than
       300 students and workers protesting at La Plaza de las Tres
       Culturas in Tlatelolco, Mexico City, in October, just weeks be-
       fore the Olympics. Jesse Owens attends the Olympics in Mexico
       City. Runners Tommie Smith and Juan Carlos give a black
       power salute when they are awarded their medals.

1969   Richard M. Nixon becomes the 37th president of the United
       States. Neil Armstrong becomes the first man to walk on the
       moon.

1971   Owens travels to the Ivory Coast April 30–May 5 at President
       Nixon's request. He conducts running clinics for youth and
       promotes the freedoms found in the United States.

1972   Owens attends the Olympics in Munich, Germany. He is
       granted an honorary doctorate of athletic arts from Ohio State.

1974   Owens is named a member of the National Track & Field Hall
       of Fame. Gerald Ford becomes the 38th president of the United
       States following Nixon's impeachment.

1975   The Fall of Saigon and the Mayaguez incident mark end to U.S.
       involvement in the Vietnam War.

1976   President Ford presents Owens with the Medal of Freedom.
       Three recreational buildings at Ohio State are named in Jesse
       Owens's honor, as well as the track in Ohio Stadium and the
       plaza outside the stadium.

1977   On August 14, Owens is inducted into the National Track &
       Field Hall of Fame. Jimmy Carter becomes the 39th president of
       the United States.

1979   Owens is diagnosed with lung cancer. President Carter awards
       him the Living Legend Award.

1980   On March 31, Jesse Owens dies. The Jesse Owens Foundation is
       created in his honor.

1981   On April 12, Owens's longtime friend Joe Louis dies.

1986   Gina Hemphill Strachan, Owens's granddaughter, carries the
       Olympic torch into the Olympic stadium in Los Angeles and
       hands it to Rafer Johnson, who ignites the flame.

1990   President George H. W. Bush awards Owens the Congressional
       Gold Medal. Ruth accepts on his behalf.

1996   On June 29, grandson Stuart Owen Rankin carries Olympic
       torch to the Jesse Owens Memorial Museum in Lawrence
       County, Alabama.

2001   The Jesse Owens Memorial Stadium for track and soccer is com-
       pleted at Ohio State.

2005   Marlene returns to Ohio State on October 14 to serve as Grand
       Marshall for the Homecoming Parade.

2006   Jesse Owens is listed third in the NCAA's list of the 100 most
       influential student-athletes, behind Jackie Robinson and Arthur
       Ashe.

Chapter 1

STRENGTH AND COURAGE IN RURAL ALABAMA

I always loved running. I wasn't very good at it, but I loved it because it was something you could do all by yourself, all under your own power. You could go in any direction, fast or slow as you wanted, fighting the wind if you felt like it, seeking out new sights just on the strength of your feet and the courage of your lungs.

—Owens 1978

The first surfaces to touch young James Cleveland Owens's feet were the wide rough-hewn shanty floorboards and the dirt-covered fields and roads of rural Lawrence County, Alabama. Born September 12, 1913, the seventh child of Henry and Emma Owens, the young boy ran whenever and wherever he could. It gave him a sense of strength, despite the fragility and weakness of his body as a result of numerous childhood illnesses, and it gave him a sense of freedom, despite of the restrictions of the covenant between poor black sharecroppers and rich white landowners. The hard times of Owens's early life in rural Alabama began to build the strength his feet would need and the courage his lungs would require as he traveled around the globe, first as an athlete, and later as a businessman and ambassador.

In September of 1913 when Owens was born, Woodrow Wilson was serving as the 28th president of the United States. Although the 50th anniversary of the Battle of Gettysburg had just been commemorated, the country was still struggling to overcome the legacy of slavery, even though slavery had been officially abolished at the end of the

Civil War. There was still great uncertainty and change in the country. Many African Americans who were formerly slaves had become poor sharecroppers on farms throughout the South, with poor whites joining them in the fields. Between 1840 and 1920, more than 37 million people immigrated to the United States—an unprecedented number—as labor and industry grew dramatically both domestically and abroad. While some people, like Andrew Carnegie and John D. Rockefeller, experienced great prosperity, the majority of Americans did not. Most labored under dangerous and difficult conditions with barely enough money to survive. There were no child labor laws to protect young children from exploitation and conditions that threatened their health and well-being. The economy was uncertain as the country went through periods of boom followed by recession. In 1913, the Sixteenth Amendment to the Constitution was ratified, allowing Congress to collect income tax, and President Wilson passed the Federal Reserve Act, which established the Federal Reserve Bank and combined business and government into a central banking system in the United States. However, neither measure stabilized or secured the economy in a way that would prevent the Great Depression that would follow just over a decade later.

Social conditions were not much better than the economic problems people faced. Jim Crow laws governed relationships between African Americans and whites throughout the country, setting up unequal and humiliating conditions for blacks just a generation away from slavery. These laws segregated African Americans from whites in public places such as restaurants, schools, theaters, and buses, and also directed people to use public facilities such as restrooms and water fountains according to the label *white* or *colored*. These segregation practices were upheld in court through laws that were the result of court cases such as *Plessy v. Ferguson* (1896), which endorsed the idea that "separate but equal" was permissible, resulting in nearly 60 more years of discrimination against African Americans.

Other social problems also prevailed at this time. Women in the United States were still not granted the right to vote, and while many entered the workforce as World War I began, they were still second-class citizens in relation to the pay, benefits, and treatment they received. The strong labor movement that began during this time attempted to change these conditions and to guarantee workers better rights, but it was a long struggle that continues to this day.

The Owens family lived in the midst of these struggles. They labored long, hard hours under difficult conditions, the slave stories of their forebears in their minds and their hopes for freedom and a better life for their children in their hearts. They inherited strength from their past for the uncertain times in which they lived.

FROM A LEGACY OF SLAVERY

The first slaves were transported to Alabama on the ship *Africane* through the port in Mobile in 1721 (ADAH 2001). Alabama had strict slavery codes that were based on the *Code Noir* (the Black Code), King Louis XIV's edict of 1685 that defined slavery and directed the conduct of slaves in French colonies until 1789. The Alabama Slavery Code of 1833 specified what was acceptable behavior for slaves. Slaves were not permitted to have guns, to learn to read or write, to be witnesses in a trial except if the case involved a slave, to leave home without a pass, or to have unlawful assemblies, among other restrictions. The laws detailed the punishment that would accompany any violation of the law.

Individual states began to ban the importation of slaves and the practice of slavery in the 1700s. The Massachusetts Constitution declared that all men were born "free and equal" in 1780, and by 1804 all northern states had declared emancipation acts. The Constitution of the United States outlawed the importation of slaves in 1808; however, slaves were still brought in illegally. By the 1860s, there were nearly four million slaves in the United States, and by 1880, the number of whites and African Americans in Alabama was nearly equal. According to the 1880 federal census, Alabama had 662,185 white and 600,103 African American residents. Children who were born to mixed-race parentage were designated as black if their mothers were black. This meant that children born to white slave owners and black slaves would continue to live in slavery. The "one drop theory" worked to categorize people as colored if they had at least one drop of non-white blood. In this way, racial categories were constructed and maintained to protect the interests of white people. From the time of slavery through the post–Civil War and Jim Crow times, people in the United States perhaps more than any other nation had been concerned with classifying citizens as white or black (Tyack 2003).

Before the Civil War, Alabama's constitution explicitly protected slavery. Alabama passed the Thirteenth Amendment (which abolished slavery) in 1865, but it would not ratify the Fourteenth Amendment (which protected equal rights for all American citizens) for three more years. This resulted in military occupation of the state, which lasted until 1876.

Alabama remained segregated and deeply divided by Jim Crow laws until the 1960s.

SHARECROPPING AND HOPES OF FREEDOM

Henry and Emma Owens's ancestors were likely transported to the United States in the 1830s (Owens 1978), which meant they were victims of illegal slave trade. In 1808, the United States banned the importation of slaves from Africa and Cuba. After this date, the importation of slaves was considered piracy, and anyone found guilty of engaging in this act could be punished with the death penalty. However, slavery continued until the Thirteenth Amendment was ratified, and the slave population continued to grow in numbers that could not be explained by reproduction alone. Since ship records were falsified at the time to disguise the exact nature of the cargo, it is hard to know exactly how many slaves were illegally transported to the United States. Some estimate that as many as 270,000 slaves were smuggled into the United States between 1820 and 1861 (Shulman 2004).

Emma's father, Phillip Fitzgerald, was the former slave of William Fitzgerald. Phillip married Parthena Alexander, another former slave. Together, the two eventually owned a sizable portion of land in Oakville, Alabama, but in an unwise business decision, a portion of the land was leased to a gin owner and subsequently lost. The remainder of the land was lost during the Great Depression when the family fell on hard economic times (McDaniel 2005b).

Henry Cleveland Owens was born in 1878, and like his wife, Emma, his parents had also been slaves. Henry's parents became sharecroppers like many other former slaves after the Civil War. Sharecroppers farmed the land for the landowners, who were typically white, and they returned crops to the landowners to pay for being able to live on the farm. Sharecroppers were very poor, and often exploited by landowners who took advantage of the fact that sharecroppers and their families needed a place to live and some way to make a living. Sharecropping was common during the Reconstruction era in the United States. It was a difficult time as people struggled to figure out how to live together since African Americans had been granted freedom, and how to sustain the U.S. economy without slavery, which was formerly a key element of economic prosperity in the United States.

Former slaves faced significant challenges concerning how they would work and organize their lives after slavery. Historian Clarence Walker explained that freed people did not want to return to work or conditions that reminded them of their former lives as slaves, but there were few work options available for them. Former slave owners and whites throughout the United States understood that cotton was still the largest U.S. export and crucial to the American economy. In addition, the United States government did not support the idea of land redistribution among former slaves, which dashed any hope of land ownership for many families. Eventually, former slaves found themselves back on plantations working cotton fields for white landowners (see PBS 2003 for more information on the Reconstruction and sharecropping).

Because plantation owners often did not have cash available to pay the field workers, they needed to develop other compensation arrangements. Most often these arrangements involved having the landowner rent a plot of land to the worker, who then became a sharecropper. In many cases, the landowner provided mules, plows, and seeds. In return, the sharecropper would live on the land and farm it, giving a percentage of the crop back to the landowner in payment. The sharecropper and his family always lived at the mercy of the landowner's arrangement. As historian Eric Foner explained, this deal between landowner and former slave served as a compromise: the former slave desired his own land, and the former slave owner desired controlled labor (PBS 2003). Poor whites also became sharecroppers, yet they did not suffer the same racial discrimination African American sharecroppers encountered through segregationist and Jim Crow laws. All sharecroppers suffered in extreme poverty. They were always vulnerable to landowners who made unfair contracts and changed agreements about crops and payments to their advantage whenever they wished.

Henry Owens grew up watching his own father work the land, trying to eke an existence from the sandy Bama soil in rural Alabama. Henry's father died early, leaving the young boy with his mule and the clothes on his back. After his father's death, Henry continued to work as a sharecropper, first for Albert Owens and then later for John Clannon (McDaniel 2005a). Although the Emancipation Proclamation and the Civil War had technically freed all slaves, freedom was not a reality for African Americans who were only one generation away from slavery in the Deep South. There were many laws and social mores that restricted their freedoms. Some restrictions, including Jim Crow laws, kept blacks from living, working, and socializing in certain places, while other restrictions involved preying on people's fears. For example, Henry never learned to read, and he was frightened of books (Owens 1970). He grew up knowing that slaves had been beaten for owning books, and that much worse could happen if they could read one. Like Henry, other former slaves and their children often lived with fears that haunted their parents and others in their communities, afraid for their safety and well-being, and concerned that the modest gains they made would be lost.

FAMILY LIFE IN OAKVILLE

From early in the morning until late at night, Henry and Emma Owens worked the farm with a mule and eventually with their children at their side, trying to sustain a meager existence on the sparse crops it produced. After Henry paid rent for the mule, the 50-acre stretch of land, and the limited equipment he had available to him, there was barely any money left. Sometimes the crops the family harvested would only make a dent in the previous years' debt. There seemed to be no way to get ahead or break out of the cycle of poverty.

The Owens family lived together in a small sharecropper's house. The shanty was constructed of rough planks that left gaps in the walls and floors, and cold air coursed in during the winter months. There was not much furniture in the house, and most of the household items were hand-made. The Owens family did not have modern amenities like running water and electricity. The children slept on blankets on the floor, making do with what they had.

The Owens family shared many sorrowful times in their shanty home. Three of Henry and Emma's young children died, and others did not survive childbirth. The family was poor, and putting food on the table was a continual struggle. Emma could serve meat to her growing family only on special occasions: birthdays, Christmas, Easter, and sometimes the Fourth of July (Owens 1978). Otherwise, they ate beans and onions, and whatever other sparse provisions they could grow in the fields or purchase on loan from the local store.

The Owens family's only reprieve from work came on Sunday. On this day, they walked nine miles to church, where services were held in the one-room schoolhouse the children sometimes attended during the week when work or illness did not interfere. The family would walk together, talking and sharing their dreams. Young James Cleveland found pleasure in these walks. He looked forward to seeing other boys his age at church, and he enjoyed the singing. He also thought that his parents seemed to have their spirits lifted when the church service ended (Owens 1978). In the afternoons, his father would race against men from other farms in the area. Henry always won (Streissguth 2006).

There were eight families who served as sharecroppers on Clannon's 250 acres of land. The Owens family had the largest plot, in part because they had the most children to help work the land. Prentice, Johnson,

Henry, Ernest, Quincy, Sylvester, and James Cleveland worked the fields, while their sisters—Ida, Josephine, and Lilly—tended the vegetable garden. Some days, young James Cleveland would pick as much as 100 pounds of cotton, depositing it into a sack as he worked. This was hard work for anyone, bending over the plants in the fields all day, with fingers bleeding and sore from extracting the cotton from the boll. More experienced cotton pickers would end up with 250–275 pounds of cotton each day, and so James Cleveland's contribution was really quite ambitious given his young age.

The Owens family also harvested vegetables, including corn and beans. After giving the landlord his share of their crops, the Owens family would split the remainder in two parts. The first part they would store for the winter, and the second part they would sell in order to buy meat or a church shirt (Owens 1978).

The Owens family's neighbors suffered just as they did, and in some cases, perhaps more. One farmer, Joe Steppart, and his wife lost every baby born to them, and the couple later hung themselves in their small shack. This devastated Henry (Owens 1970). He and Joe were close in age and the two had begun to work as sharecroppers at the same time. Over the years, Henry had tried to help Joe to be more successful in his farming, even allowing some of his sons to help with the work. But ultimately it was to no avail. Joe could not continue the struggle. It was a painful loss for the Owens family and the Oakville community.

Oakville, where the Owens family lived, was eight miles from Decatur, Alabama, in the northern part of the state. There was not much in Oakville beyond the farmland and a small grocery store owned by a white man. The Owens family tried to avoid using the store as much as they could. It only increased their debts. Often Henry and his son Prentice would wake up earlier than usual to try to shoot some rabbits for dinner, and Emma tried to maintain a small vegetable garden near the house for food. Yet this was not enough to feed a large family, and so the storekeeper kept a sheet of paper to record the debt the family accrued over the year. In December, after the crops were in, he tallied the debt and determined what was owed. Often, the family found it was sinking deeper into debt, and since no one could read or check the calculations on the bill, there was no way to know the extent to which they were being cheated (Owens 1970).

Times were difficult. In 1915, the boll weevil devastated cotton fields throughout Alabama. Up to this time, cotton was the major crop in Alabama. In 1909, 3.7 million acres of cotton were farmed in Alabama, and the crop accounted for 60.3 percent of the total crop values for the state (Center for Business and Economic Research 1999). World War I created a larger demand for farmers to produce food crops, a trend that continued throughout the Great Depression, and eventually the mechanization of farm work decreased the number of farm hands needed to work the land. By 1913, more than 10,000 steam engines were used to thresh wheat on large farms. These were rapidly replaced as the manufacture and design of farm tractors improved. Although John Froelich built the first gas-powered tractor in Iowa in 1892, only two were sold. However, the design was improved by the Waterloo Gasoline Traction Engine Company, and by 1917, Henry Ford began to mass produce the Fordson tractor, which was sold in the United States, Ireland, England, and Russia. By the 1920s, the declining economy influenced farm prices, and the war impacted the number of laborers available for farm work. Many farmers began to turn toward mechanized solutions such as tractors to help them compensate for these demands. During this same time period, many African American farmers began to migrate north to find jobs in factories and industry.

In 1920, when the Owens family had a particularly good cotton crop, it looked like times might change. They hoped they would at last be able to get out of debt. When Clannon realized this, he called Henry to his home, where Clannon's assistant explained that he was going to change the sharecropping deal. Rather than splitting the profit on the crops 50–50, he was going to change their agreement to 60–40. When Henry explained that the new deal was unfair and asked how he was supposed to provide a good life for his sons so they could get ahead, the assistant replied that Henry should be glad to have his sons survive. Beyond that, he assured Henry that his boys would never amount to anything (Owens 1970).

Owens later explained that his family lived in a constant state of fear, fear of Clannon and what he could do to them. They felt isolated and vulnerable, unable to change their condition no matter how hard they work. For the Owens family and millions of other African American families throughout the United States in the 1910s, "not starving was the best you could do" (Owens 1978, 10–11).

YOUNG J. C.

As a young boy, most people called James Cleveland "J. C.," except for his mother and father. To Emma, this young boy was her "gift child," born when she thought she could no longer have any more children. To Henry, he was "Buster." By all accounts, J. C. was a rambunctious child, who ran and played and even got into trouble on occasion. Sometimes his older brothers had to help him out of a bind. One notable time they rescued him when he got into a fight with a Clannon boy who called his mother a name.

The older Owens boys arrived on the scene just as the Clannon brothers were about to carve their initials on the scared child's face. In spite of the mischief J. C. generated, there was only one time that the trouble he caused resulted in his father spanking him. One Sunday, J. C. carved some soap to look like an onion and his mother put it in the Sunday stew. That day, no one in the Owens family had anything to eat (Owens 1978).

J. C. was often sick as a child, and for several winters in a row he contracted pneumonia. There were times when his family was sure he would not survive, but somehow the boy miraculously pulled through. Frail as he may have appeared, he had an inner strength and determination that helped him to overcome insurmountable odds, even as a very young child.

As though his struggle with constant bouts of pneumonia was not hard enough on the young boy, another illness almost took young J. C.'s life. Just after he turned five years of age, a bump formed on his chest. As it grew, it became increasingly harder for the young boy to breathe. The nearest doctor was 75 miles away in Birmingham, but that did not matter. The family could never afford to pay a doctor. Emma was not willing to stand by and let her young son die, so she decided to use a knife to extract the bump from his frail and failing body. As his family stood by his bedside, Emma began to cut the bump out of J. C. Eventually the young boy lapsed into unconsciousness, waking to find his family still at home watching over him. No one worked the fields that day, a clear indication of how serious his situation was. Young J. C. was sure he was going to die. Although his mother was able to remove the entire lump from his small body, she was not able to stop the bleeding from the deep wound. J. C.'s mother and father tried everything they could to stop the bleeding, but nothing seemed to work. As Emma kept vigil at his bedside, young J. C. faded in and out of consciousness, and the bleeding would not stop.

As Owens later told the story, he recalled how on the third night after "the cutting," he heard his father praying for him outside the front door of their house. He recalled his father's desperate, humble prayer:

> Oh Lord Jesus ... please ... please hear me. ... I know you hears everything ... but this ... saving ... means everything. ... She'll die if he dies—and if she dies, Lord, we'll all die—all of us. ... He's my last boy—J. C.'s the one you gave me last to carry my name—she'll die if you take him from me—she always said he was born special—she said he was made when he couldn't be. ... Please don't take him from me, Lord—I'll do anything—the hardest thing—anything to pay you back. (Owens 1978, 15–16)

J. C. got out of bed, blood trickling out of the open wound in his chest, and went to his father. As he crawled through the door to him, his father gathered him in his arms and told him to pray. J. C. was not sure what to say in his prayer, but he knelt beside his father and prayed. Then his father carried him back into the house, and the bleeding stopped. Young J. C. was weakened, but he would survive.

TOUGH DECISIONS

On Christmas Day in 1920, when J. C. was just seven years of age, there was no meat on the table, no Christmas tree in the corner, and no hopeful talk about how the next year would be better during the nine-mile walk home from church. Usually the family shared their dreams with one another as they made their way to and from church, and they often laughed when young J. C. told them he wanted to go to college some day. But there would be no dreaming today. Times were tough and they promised to only get worse.

When the Owens family returned to their home, the somber mood continued. No one wanted to play games with young J. C. Instead, his parents went out to the fields to talk about their life and their future on the farm in Oakville. Curious about what was going on, J. C. trailed behind without his parents knowing to eavesdrop on their conversation. He learned that they were considering something important, but he could not figure out what it was. When his parents discovered that J. C. had followed them, they made him go home. When Henry and Emma finally returned, they had an announcement for the family: they were going to move north to find a better life. Their daughter Lilly had already moved to Cleveland in search of work, and she wrote letters back to her parents about the possibilities they could find in the North. It was a risky decision. The family knew what their life was in Alabama. There were so many unknowns about moving north. There was much they would leave behind, including the land that Henry and his father and grandfather before him had farmed. But the Stepparts' tragic deaths, J. C.'s constant illnesses, and Clannon's ruthless ways contributed to the final decision to move north. Henry was 42 years of age, a difficult time to embark on such a change, but he knew he had to do something to realize a different life for his wife and children.

J. C. sold the mule to Clannon, his brothers returned the few farm tools, and his mother and sisters scrubbed the house. The Owens family earned only $24 for their possessions (Owens 1972). Clannon did not pay them well, in part because he wanted to keep them where they were. It was difficult to find someone who could farm as well as Henry and his sons (Owens 1970). After everything was sold, the family packed the few remaining items they owned. The Owens family left their home and all they knew before sundown, taking the train to the North where they would find a new life and new dreams. The traveled as far north as they could, coincidentally ending up in the city that Henry and young J. C. had as a middle name: Cleveland.

Chapter 2

THE OWENS FAMILY
MOVES TO OHIO

Going north was the hardest thing for [my father] to do . . . he
was cut off from everything he had known.

—*Owens 1978, 27*

When the Owens family boarded the train, they left everything and
everyone they knew behind. The family stayed on the train until they
arrived in Cleveland, where they would make a new life. The city was significantly different from their former home in rural Alabama. Now they
were in Cuyahoga County in Ohio, on the southern shores of Lake Erie,
living in a city that boasted the fifth-largest population in the United
States (numbering nearly 800,000 in 1920). Because it was located near
the Cuyahoga River, the Ohio and Erie canals, and several railway lines,
Cleveland had become a major industrial center. Rockefeller's Standard
Oil Company had come to dominate the Cleveland area. The Owens
family would need to learn to adapt to the much colder weather and lake-
effect snow that came with the harsh Cleveland winters. They would also
need to adjust to urban life, with its public transportation and neighborhoods swarming with people.

The Owens family was not the only sharecropping family to move north
during this time. Between 1914 and 1950, millions of African American
families moved from the South to large industrial cities like New York,
Detroit, Philadelphia, Baltimore, St. Louis, and Chicago. Some also relocated to Los Angeles or other smaller cities. In the two decades between
1910 and 1930, Cleveland's population alone grew by 307 percent (Digital
History 2006). This mass movement of African Americans into northern

cities became known as the Great Migration. The migration occurred due to a variety of factors, including failed crops and the significant difficulties people faced trying to sustain decent lives as sharecroppers. Moving to the North provided new opportunities for work that could pay a living wage and hope that families could rise from the extreme poverty they faced in the South. Throughout this time, there was a growing need for industrial workers in the North as a result of wartime demands. In addition to jobs, the North promised to offer a different and perhaps safer way of life. Continued lynchings and increasingly restrictive Jim Crow laws in the Deep South made life unbearable and even dangerous. While there was still racism and discrimination in the North, African Americans would not suffer as much in these cities as they had in the Deep South.

Yet, the move to the North was not without problems. Housing became a source of difficulty for many African American families during this time, with whites often resorting to restrictive covenants to prevent homeowners from selling their houses to African American families (Digital History 2006). This resulted in African Americans living in neighborhoods together, creating cities within cities, the most famous of which was Harlem in New York City. The Owens family found a house to rent in Cleveland, one that was large enough to accommodate the entire family. Emma organized the schedule so that everyone could work as much as possible, but she made sure that there was always someone at home to take care of whoever else might be home (Owens 1978).

After the Owens family relocated, most of the family members were successful in finding work in Cleveland. They did not find prestigious or high-paying jobs waiting for them, but at least there was some way to earn money. Emma and the girls worked as maids, with the girls earning $0.20 an hour and Emma earning $0.30. When adjusted for inflation, this would translate to roughly $2.36 and $3.20 per hour in 2006. The Owens women were clearly working very hard to earn a small amount of money, but their earnings alone would not be enough to sustain the family. Yet the women persevered. Owens later wrote in his autobiography that his mother never became tired, and she would not let her daughters become tired either. Instead, they would work and earn as much as they could to sustain the family.

The Owens boys found work where they could, sometimes unloading freight trains or working part-time as janitors. They were used to hard labor after spending their lives working from sunup to sundown in the fields in Alabama. Although they never had much money, together the family could earn more than they would have ever cobbled together on Clannon's farm. J. C. reported that in time he owned three shirts, rather than just one for church and one for everyday, and the family enjoyed meat on the table at least one time each week (Owens 1978). After a year, Emma Owens saved enough money to buy a small Bible with silver letters, a valued treasure she kept on a special shelf by the fireplace in their home (Owens 1970).

Life in Cleveland was perhaps most difficult for Henry Owens. He experienced the most trouble finding a job and worried about providing for his family. Henry was over 40 years of age, and he could not read or write or even recognize his own name in print. Henry spent most of his time looking for a job, sometimes finding work as a garbage collector or something else temporary in nature. While he never complained, the family knew that this was hard on a man who wanted to support his family financially. At least in Oakville he had been the primary provider. After the family moved to Cleveland, he would never have steady work again.

OFF TO SCHOOL

After the family moved north, J. C. began to attend a new school in Cleveland, Bolton Elementary School. His brothers Prentice and Quincy walked the young boy to school on the first two days, but by the third day J. C., who was only eight years old at the time, had to walk alone. His brothers found jobs and they needed to go to work, so they could no longer escort their little brother to his school building. On his first day walking to school alone, J. C. lost his way. Each new street looked unfamiliar to the boy, and the experience must have been frightening, but he kept trying and eventually found the school building.

Since J. C. was late to class, he had to get a special note when he finally arrived. The teacher who provided the note was named Charles Riley. Riley talked with the young boy. The teacher seemed to be understanding about why J. C. was late for school; certainly the child was not the first son of sharecroppers to attend Bolton Elementary. Yet Riley could not help but notice with concern that this child was thinner than the other children of southern sharecroppers (Owens 1972). J. C. had to explain to the friendly man that he had been sick quite often before he moved to Cleveland, but that he was going to survive. Riley told the boy he would need to run to keep surviving, particularly in the cold Cleveland winters. Little did Riley know at the time how prescient his advice would be.

J. C.'s formal education in Alabama had been sporadic at best, but now he looked forward to regularly attending classes at the school. The young boy still held onto his dream of going to college one day, even though this may have seemed like an impossibility to most people. Bolton Elementary

School was desegregated, like other schools in the North, which was another new experience for the boy. J. C. sat side by side for the first time with white and African American children alike. Although everything was strange and new to the boy, he remained full of hope.

The first day of school brought changes J. C. could never have anticipated. One change happened almost immediately. As attendance was taken, the teacher misunderstood the boy's southern accent. When she asked for his name, he replied J. C., but she thought he said Jesse. Young J. C. was too embarrassed to correct her, and so from that moment on he became known as Jesse. This was his new northern name, an unexpected part of his new northern life. Everyone he knew began to call him Jesse; everyone, that is, except his father. Henry would always call his youngest son J. C. or his old nickname from Alabama, Buster.

Other changes as a result of beginning school were not so immediate, but he met people who would change his life forever. When he entered the fifth grade, Owens became better acquainted with Charles Riley, the kindly teacher who signed J. C.'s late pass on the first morning he walked to school alone. Riley was a high school coach who also taught gym classes at Owens's elementary school. Riley saw the boy playing on the playground, and noticed his running ability. Riley approached Owens and asked if he would be interested in joining the track team. Owens later wrote that Riley approached him not because he saw a potential athlete, but instead because he saw a "potential corpse" (Owens 1970, 101). Owens was enthusiastic about Riley's proposition, even though he felt he was not particularly talented.

Owens agreed to practice with Riley, but he could not stay after school to run because he needed to keep his jobs. After school, he ran errands and made deliveries for a nearby grocery store, and he also worked one day each week in a greenhouse. Even though he was young and attending school, he needed to contribute to the family income as best as he could. At one point he traveled eight miles to a shoe-shining parlor each day after school to earn some money for his family (Clowser 1952). He was the only member of his family who was still attending school, and the family, struggling within the context of the Great Depression, wondered if he should drop out of school to take a full-time job. Owens's mother persuaded them otherwise, and the boy remained in school (Clowser 1952).

Since Owens could not quit his jobs, Riley agreed to meet him for an hour before school each morning so they could work on his running techniques and exercise routine. The coach had the boy run up and down the sidewalk, and although Owens still appeared to be quite thin, running helped to develop his strength and stamina. Coach Riley did more than teach Owens to run. He brought him much-needed food, and he often took Owens to his home on Sundays so that the boy could eat a nice meal that Mrs. Riley prepared. As they worked together, Owens grew stronger and noticeably more athletic.

Owens later wrote that Riley was the first white man he really knew, and he gave Owens hope that there were other white men like him who would understand and love African Americans (Owens 1970). Riley was the same age as Owens's father—nearly 50 years old when they met. Riley had two sons of his own, but one did not like sports, and the other was born with a physical disability (McRae 2002, 50). Riley took Owens under his wing and treated him as a member of his own family. The coach taught Owens many lessons about life, not through lectures, but by asking careful questions and making observations that forced Owens to think things through on his own.

One particular piece of advice Riley offered to Owens made all the difference to him (Owens 1970). When Owens was thinking about quitting the track team early in his training, Riley told him that he was not training for next week, or next month, or even next year. He instead told him that he should practice as though he were training for four years from next Friday. Through this advice, Owens came to understand that he was working toward something he would realize in the future, and that he was not expected to change overnight. He began to enjoy running, but he still needed to learn how to win.

FALLING IN LOVE

Shortly after he started school, Owens met another person who would change his life forever. There was a girl who caught the young boy's eye. Her name was Minnie Ruth Solomon. Owens claimed that he fell in love with her the very first time they talked, and each time they talked after that he fell in love with her more and more. Ruth was beautiful, and Owens later wrote that although Ruth was as poor as he was, he found her to be untouched by this and free from prejudice (Owens 1978).

Ruth was born in Locust Grove, Georgia on April 27, 1915, and her family migrated to the north in search of a better life, just as the Owens family had. After Owens met the young girl, he gave her sister a note, asking her to pass it on to Ruth. The note contained a short message: "I want to walk you home" (Wallace 1986). Ruth agreed, and the young boy began to regularly meet Ruth after school to walk her home and carry her books. Even though they were only in fourth grade at the time, Owens asked Ruth to marry him (Owens 1978). She agreed. Although it would be nearly a decade until they were married, the two were committed to one another from their childhood years until the end of their lives. They stood by each other through good times and bad times.

LEARNING TO WIN

Jesse Owens went to East Technical High School in 1930. Soon after, he began to compete with the track team against students from other schools. His first official competition, which came three years after he began to train with Riley, was a quarter-mile run. Coach Riley had him training at this distance so that the 220- and 100-yard races would seem much shorter. Owens wanted to win, and he started the race strong. Yet, just 100 yards into the race, his competitors began to close on him. The older and more experienced runners passed Owens, and he lost the race, coming in fourth place. Although he was not happy about this loss, it turned out to be a memorable learning experience for Owens.

The next Sunday, Riley told Owens he was going to take him to see some of the world's best runners. He wanted him to learn something about how to win by running other racers down, not staring them down (Owens 1978). Much to Owens's surprise, the two ended up at a horse track where they studied the winning horses' face and body movements. Owens claimed he learned a great deal that day. He learned that the winning horses made it look easy to win, even if it was not, because they kept their determination on the inside. He also learned that he was an athlete, not an actor, and that he should never stare down the other runners in a race. Instead, he should look straight ahead and run the race. Owens never forgot these lessons.

Another important lesson that Riley taught Owens was that he had to beat himself every time he raced. When Owens ran the 220-yard dash for the first time against other Cleveland-area high school students, he was one of two runners that Riley entered in the race. Owens ran his hardest, internalizing the many things he learned from watching the racehorses compete. He did not come in first place in that race, in spite of the determination and effort he put into his running. Yet, when the race was over, Riley congratulated Owens because he knew how hard he had run. Even after he crossed the finish line, Owens kept running. Riley saw this determination and he knew that Owens would be a champion (Owens 1978).

Owens's family stood behind him as he pursued his interests in track and field, in large part because Emma always supported her son, no matter what he wished to do (McDaniel 2005b). The Owens family placed hope in the boy, doing everything they could to help him to stay in school, be successful, and perhaps realize the dream he expressed when he was a young man in Alabama about wanting to go to college. Yet Owens's early dreams were limited by his lack of experience with the broader world outside of Oakville. As a young child, he was unaware of the Olympics and the possibility of winning a gold medal. Those dreams were yet to come.

Jesse Owens first learned about the Olympic Games when he was a high school student in 1932 and he read about the games in the newspaper. Around the same time, Olympic champion Charlie Paddock visited Owens's high school to speak with students about what it was like to be in the Olympics (Owens 1976). Paddock won gold medals in the 1920 Olympics in Antwerp in the 100-meter race and 4 × 100-meter relay. He also won a silver medal in the 200-meter race. In addition to these accomplishments, Paddock qualified for the 1924 Olympics in Paris, where he won a silver medal in the 200-meter race. Paddock was known for his flying finishes as he leaped through the air to cross the finish line first. Because of his speed and the records he held in the 100-meter and 100-yard dashes in the 1920s, Paddock was the first person to be called the World's Fastest Human. Paddock ran the 100 meter in 10.4 seconds, a time Owens would beat just a few years later in Chicago in 1936. Although Paddock did not beat Jim Thorpe's 1912 Olympic record of 10.0 seconds for the 100-meter race in Stockholm, Thorpe's record was later revoked because he had formerly played semipro baseball and was disqualified as an amateur athlete.

When Charlie Paddock visited Owens's school, Coach Riley had Owens meet with the Olympian in Riley's office. Owens was impressed with Paddock, and he decided that he also wanted to be the world's fastest human. Riley told the boy that it would take determination, dedication, and discipline, and he encouraged Owens to pursue his dreams (Owens 1976).

After this, Owens trained harder. He ran faster, jumped farther, and began to become accustomed to winning. He was competing with himself to become better and better as an athlete. This inner drive would propel him through many high school victories, breaking records held by other high school and college athletes. Throughout his high school years, Owens still held down jobs after school as he kept up his training schedule. He was determined to keep winning.

Track and field was a relatively new sport for high schools when Owens trained with Coach Riley. Most track and field events began across Ohio in the 1890s, and schools were regularly participating, usually on a county-wide basis, with girls' and boys' meets held separately. Track and field events tended to be desegregated since schools in Ohio were desegregated. African American athletes competed for their schools alongside their white peers.

The first state meet for Ohio high schools was held on May 23, 1908, sponsored by Denison University in Granville (Ohio High School Athletic Association). The meet was originally an invitational, and in subsequent years it was probably held at various universities. After the 1920 meet, the meet ceased to be an invitational and came under directly the Ohio High School Athletic Association's control. East Technical won several important track meets in 1932 and 1933, when Owens was on the team and making significant contributions to the team's overall score. Owens competed with some remarkable athletes at these events. On June 11, 1932, the *New York Times* reported that out of 200 athletes, including high school and college stars, Owens shared the spotlight with a Miss Stella Walsh of Cleveland. Walsh sprinted 50 meters in 6.4 seconds, tying the world record for the race. Walsh also ran the 100 meter in 12.1 seconds, which matched the world record at that time, and she threw a discus 127 feet, 4 inches, shattering the Amateur Athletic Union (AAU) record of 107 feet, 6 inches. At the same event, Owens earned significant attention for running the 100 meter in 10.3 seconds, beating Charlie Paddock's world record by a full second. The judges did not officially recognize Owens's record, however, because they felt there was a strong wind at Owens's back (*New York Times* 1932).

Another big track and field meet in Ohio at that time was the Mansfield Relays. Competing in this event on April 22, 1933, Owens tied the national interscholastic record for the 100-yard dash (9.6 seconds), even though the *New York Times* reported that he was running against the wind. Owens also won the 200-yard dash and the broad jump at this meet.

Just a month later in May of 1933, Owens competed at the Interscholastic Championships in Chicago, Illinois. In front of one of the largest audiences he had seen, Owens jumped 24 feet, 9⅗ inches to win the event. He ran in his seemingly effortless way to win the 100-yard race in 9.4 seconds, and the 200-yard race in 20.7 seconds. These records stood for high school competitions until 1954 (Mandell 1987).

Then in June of 1933, Owens achieved his biggest success to date at the National Interscholastic Track and Field Championship held at Soldier Field in Chicago. East Technical High School won the championship with 54 points, 30 of which were earned by Owens. Coming in second place that day was North High, of Wichita, Kansas, with 35 points. Owens officially beat the world record in the 100 meter, finishing in first place with a record time of 9.4 seconds. He beat the world record formerly held by Frank Wykoff by 0.2 second. That same day, Owens beat the scholastic mark for the long jump by leaping 24 feet, 9½ inches (7 inches further than the previous record). Owens also won the 220-yard dash in 20.7 seconds,

0.4 second faster than the former scholastic record, and 0.1 second faster than the world record held by Roland Locke of Nebraska (*New York Times* 1933).

Sportswriters were paying attention to the young athlete, putting Owens in the headlines for their stories and calling attention to the remarkable accomplishments of this "school boy." As he finished high school, his name was easily recognized by those who followed track and field events. He had learned how to win. The wide publicity his victories received meant that Owens was on the brink of realizing his childhood dream of going to college. He had the attention of university track coaches across the country, and he began to get offers from various colleges.

As this was all a new experience for Owens and his family, he sought out advice from his long-term coach and mentor, Charles Riley. When Owens went to see his coach, Riley advised him to pay his own way through college, making it clear that he was an amateur athlete. Definitions of amateurism were quite strict, and if he did not accept money for tuition or college this would keep the possibility of competing in the Olympics open to him. Owens decided to take his coach's advice. As the meeting came to an end, Riley passed on a poem called "Excelsior," by Henry Wadsworth Longfellow. The poem was about determination, perseverance, and striving to be better, lessons that would serve Owens well over his lifetime. Owens held onto the poem, and he later used it as a structure to organize his autobiography, *Jesse: The Man Who Outran Hitler*.

Years later, in this autobiography, Owens reflected on the family's move to Cleveland. He realized that they had gained a great deal by moving north, but he also noticed there were things they had lost. Among them, the family did not attend church every Sunday, as they had in Oakville, and they no longer talked together about their dreams, as they had when they walked home from church in Alabama. Instead, like many other American families struggling to survive through the Great Depression and its aftermath, they became caught up in trying to make ends meet and working as much as they could to put food on the table and clothes on their backs. They had a difficult life, but Owens's victories and the potential for him to succeed in the future gave the family great hope. Owens was extremely popular and people from all walks of life came to see him race. He had a crowd-pleasing personality and easy smile. As his high school career came to an end, his future looked extremely bright.

Chapter 3

THE BUCKEYE BULLET

God has given everyone the ability to do something. It might
be as a musician or a painter, a businessman or a teacher. He
gave me ability to compete in track and field.

—Owens 1976, 114

Jesse Owens would finally be able to realize his childhood dream. Given
his high school accomplishments in track and field, it was certain that
when he graduated he would go to college. Owens's successful record on
the East Technical High School track team meant that his name and
accomplishments were well recognized among university track coaches
across the country. Newspapers throughout the Northeast carried stories
of his victories, including major newspapers like the *New York Times*.
While Jesse Owens could have chosen from any number of universities,
he decided to attend The Ohio State University in Columbus. The school
had an excellent track and field program, and the coach, Larry Snyder,
was known for his progressive ideas.

Owens's decision to attend Ohio State was likely influenced by his
wish to be near his family as well. In Columbus, Owens would be less
than 200 miles from his family, including his childhood sweetheart Ruth.
By this time, Owens and Ruth had a baby daughter together, and it was
important for him to be as close to them as possible. Gloria was born on
August 8, 1932, just as Owens was starting his senior year of high school.
Ruth and the baby lived with her parents as Owens finished his studies at
East Technical High School. When he went to college, Ruth and Gloria
would continue to live with her parents. Ruth held a job in a beauty salon

to help support herself and the baby, and Ruth's parents looked after the child when Ruth was working.

It would not be easy for Owens to visit home after he moved to Columbus since his schedule was very full and he did not have a car. But he would be able to take the train or the bus home on his holiday and semester breaks. A bus ride between Cleveland and Columbus would take about three hours. He knew he would need to save his money to afford the fare, and he was willing to hold down any number of jobs while he was a student to cover his expenses. Owens wanted to make his family proud of him. It was because of their support that he was able to realize this dream. His family, especially his mother, had insisted that he stay in school, even though they could have used the money he would have earned had he worked full time. His accomplishments were important to them, and they hoped his talent on the track field would bring him some different choices in life than they had been offered. The idea of going to college may have seemed unreachable as the family walked the dusty Alabama roads when Owens was a young boy, but now this dream was becoming a reality. He would be a Buckeye.

THE OHIO STATE UNIVERSITY

The Ohio State University was founded in 1870 as The Ohio Agricultural and Mechanical College. As a land-grant institution, Ohio State was originally funded through the Morrill Act of 1862, which granted 30,000 acres of federal land per state to make higher education accessible and practical to residents. While classical studies were included in the curriculum, they were not the primary focus for land-grant institutions. Instead, these schools were intended to emphasize agriculture, military tactics, and engineering.

When Owens started his college education, he planned to major in physical education. Beginning in 1917, Ohio law required that physical and health education be taught in its public schools, and teachers were needed to fill these positions. Through the 1920s, Ohio State saw increases in enrollment in physical- and teacher-education programs as a result. It was also around this time that these education programs at Ohio State went from two-year to four-year programs. Owens looked forward to finding a job that would combine his love for track and field with his interest in young people. He hoped to become a teacher and coach so that he could have a positive influence on young people in the same way his teachers and coach influenced him.

The Ohio State University had a well-established track and field program by the time Owens enrolled. The first Ohio Intercollegiate

Athletic Association (OIAA) track meet was held at Ohio State on May 31, 1884. At the time, events included the 22-pound shot put, the two-mile go-as-you-please race, the standing high jump, the 50-yard hop, and the baseball throw. When Owens joined the team, there was a strong and consistent commitment from the university to the track and field program, and some of the best training and equipment of the time was available to these athletes. The track was cinder, with the top layer made of residue from the iron-smelting process (Rooney 1984). As they ran, runners would kick up chunks of the track (Daley 1971). Unlike today, there were no starting blocks for runners. Instead, Owens and his teammates had to use a small trowel to dig holes in the track behind the starting line. A runner would put his toes in the hole to help give him a better start to the race. Sometimes the holes would give way, particularly if the ground was wet, causing problems for the runners at the start of the race.

Other areas of track and field were also different at that time. High jumpers did not have soft, raised landings to break their fall; instead, they landed in sand pits and other surfaces that were much harder than we have today. Because of this, some early jumpers used methods that allowed them to land in a more upright fashion when possible. Early high jumpers often approached the bar either straight on, similar to a hurdler, or using a scissors technique, where the jumper would approach the bar at a diagonal and throw his legs over it in a scissoring motion. American high jumper M. F. Horine later developed what became known as a Western roll, a technique where the inner leg leads in the jump so that the athlete's body becomes flattened as it goes over the bar. This method was the most widely used in the 1936 Berlin Olympics, and it was the choice of American Cornelius Johnson, who won a gold medal with a winning jump of 6 feet, 9¾ inches.

CONTROVERSY AND CHALLENGES AT OHIO STATE

Jesse Owens's decision to go to Ohio State was controversial among the African American community. Ohio State was not desegregated, and at the time Owens enrolled, the university was well known for its racial prejudices. There were very few African Americans among the student body, even though gains were being made in this area. At the time he enrolled there were approximately 100 African American students, up significantly from perhaps 10 students a decade earlier (Mandell 1987). However, the number was still quite small—less than 1 percent of the overall university enrollment of approximately 15,000 students.

Many of the African American students who attended Ohio State were athletes. Yet despite the increased number of African American students, they still faced significant discrimination, even on sports teams. Ohio State's head football coach Francis Schmidt did not play any African American athletes on the Ohio State team when he led the Buckeyes from 1934–1940. Talented African American athletes like Bill Willis, one of the most famous African American professional football players in the 1940s and 1950s, entered the university expecting to join the track team rather than the football team because of these racist practices. Willis's opportunities changed when a new coach led the team beginning in 1941, and he ended up on the team, later contributing to its 1942 Western Conference Championship.

Owens certainly encountered racism at Ohio State, as he would have at any integrated major university at the time. Had he gone to school in the South, Owens would only have been able to attend an all-black university. Although in the North he was able to attend Ohio State, his experiences were clearly segregated along racial lines. Owens would not be able to live on campus as the other white students did, and he would not be able to eat with other track athletes who were white. There was only one male dorm for students, and this was for the white students. Owens would need to live with other African American students in a boarding house a mile from campus (Raatma 2004).

In addition to his segregated experiences on campus, Owens encountered difficulty while traveling as an African American member of the university's track team. The African American teammates had to ride together in a car, separate from the white members of the team, who rode in their own cars. Owens realized this was not fair, and while he complied, he also resented the treatment he faced (Owens 1970). While he acknowledged that not every white teammate was prejudiced against him, he was offended by the differential treatment that was part of his daily life. In addition to being unable to ride in a car with other members of his team, Owens was not permitted to take showers with white teammates, or to eat in restaurants with them on the way to a track event. Owens told of times when the white members of the team would bring food out to the car where the African Americans waited, yet even these gestures were sometimes thwarted. Owens later recalled how a restaurant owner in Indiana came to the car to take the food away from the African American boys when he realized where the white athletes were taking the food. Owens had to go to the meet on an empty stomach. Although Owens did not get to eat that day, just like many other days when restaurants would not serve him, he still won the meet, and felt that he defeated that white restaurant owner and others like him. When whites approached him for his autograph, he thought about how he was able to win in spite of the racism many whites held.

People in his community were well aware of the racism he would face when he attended Ohio State, and some tried to persuade him to go to a different school. When Owens's decision to go to Ohio State was finalized and made public, the *Chicago Defender*, one of the most respected African American newspapers of the time, conveyed the outrage many people felt: "Owens will be an asset to any school. So why help an institution that majors in prejudice? . . . You must realize, Jesse, that in the age in which you are living, a militant spirit against prejudice in all its forms must be shown. The day has passed for turning the cheek. We must fight or perish under the iron heel of the oppressor" (as quoted in McRae 2002, 53).

Owens clearly had different views about the possibilities Ohio State could offer. Rather than avoid the institution because of racial prejudice, he decided to go there to see what the university and track team could offer him, and perhaps to see whether he could make a difference at the institution. This position—that he could try to make things better through his involvement—was key to his philosophy about race in the years to come.

When Owens started his studies at Ohio State, there were no athletic scholarships available for him. Owens had to pay his own tuition, room, and board. He did this by working various jobs when he was not required to be in class. At first, he worked from four to eleven thirty p.m. each evening as a freight-elevator operator at the State of Ohio Office Building. Racism even permeated his employment experience. White students would operate elevators in the front of the building because these were the elevators that people rode. These operators would make sure that people moved safely on and off the elevator, and they would answer questions about which floors people needed. Owens was not permitted to operate these elevators. Instead, he had to work the freight elevators in the back of the building. He did not seem to mind this too much, though. He was able to study during slow times on his shift.

During his student years, Owens held many different jobs. Sometimes he worked at the school library, and sometimes as a table waiter for the white students. He pumped gas for Wright's Sohio Service Station in East Cleveland when he was in high school, and he returned to this job during his breaks from the university. While the jobs Owens held were never prestigious, he always seemed to be glad to have a job because it gave him the chance to go to college and to earn some money. In time, Owens found a better-paying and higher-profile job working as a page at the Ohio

House of Representatives. Here he would run messages and papers to various offices in the capital building. The young man who had once picked 100 pounds of cotton a day as a young and sickly boy was not afraid to work, especially if it could mean a chance at a different life for himself and his family.

THE TRACK TEAM

Larry Snyder, a white man who Owens later described as colorblind, was his new coach at the university. Snyder began his coaching career at Ohio State in 1932, just before Owens arrived. Prior to that, he had earned accolades for his own accomplishments as a high hurdler on the track team at Ohio State. Snyder was experienced and knowledgeable about track, and he quickly earned the respect of the young men he coached.

Coach Snyder quickly recognized Owens's talent, but he also knew there was room for improvement in his running and long jump. Owens certainly had a unique running style. Coach Riley had taught him to run as though he was dancing on hot coals, and Owens took his coach's instruction seriously. When he ran, it almost seemed that his feet never touched the ground. Snyder taught Owens to crouch more compactly at the starting line so that he could get a faster start, and this became a remarkable strength in Owens's racing. If he failed to get a strong start, he risked losing the race to other more powerful runners. Once his race was underway, he had a straight up posture that allowed him to take in more air with each breath. No matter how difficult the race was Owens always had an easy style, like it was completely effortless for him to run. Some observers said that it seemed like he did not run at all. Instead, "he floated, almost like a disembodied spirit" (Daley 1936, 53).

Snyder taught Owens new skills for his long jump as well. He taught Owens to pump his arms and legs in the air as he jumped so that he would add more distance to his leaps. Soon Owens seemed to soar through the air, arms and legs in motion, gaining inches as he mastered these new techniques.

Owens responded well to the new training Snyder provided. In the 1934 Big Ten Freshmen meet held in Columbus, Owens won all three events he entered, setting new conference records in each. He ran the 100-yard dash in 9.6 seconds, the 220 in 21.0 seconds, and he jumped 24 feet, 10 inches in the long jump. No doubt his new coach was pleased to have Owens on the team. The two developed a close relationship, and they often engaged in pre-competition inspirational talks that sometimes brought tears to both of their eyes (Mandell 1987).

Owens had many good friends who were also world-class competitors on his team. Dave Albritton, a high jumper who was one of the first to use a straddle technique, met Owens at Fairmount Junior High School. The two would be lifelong friends. Dave and Owens had much in common. They had lived just four miles away from one another in Alabama, even though they were not acquainted at the time. The boys' families both migrated to Cleveland around the same time and with similar goals—to have a better life. The two competed on the track teams for their high school and college teams, and they shared many victories together on and off the field. Albritton referred to Owens as Shorty, milking the fact that at 6 feet 1 inch he was a few inches taller than Owens, who was 5 feet 10¾ inches.

The two friends decided to split the cost of a 1914 Model T Ford so they could get to track meets. They knew they could never ride in the same car with their white teammates. The dilapidated vehicle cost them each $16.25, money they scraped together from various jobs they each held in addition to going to school and competing on the team (Owens 1970).

Ralph Metcalfe, who attended Marquette University in Milwaukee, Wisconsin, was one of Owens's toughest competitors. While the two were in college, Metcalfe also became one of his closest friends. Owens first ran against Metcalfe in the 1933 AAU meet. Metcalfe had just won silver and bronze metals in the 1932 Olympics in Los Angeles. He was a sure pick for the 1936 Olympics, and at the time the two men competed, Owens was only in high school. It was a tight race, and Owens lost by a slight margin. After the race, the two runners congratulated one another. Owens admitted that he thought he had Metcalfe beat, and Metcalfe replied "Maybe that's what beat you, Jesse" (Owens 1972, 81). Owens remembered these words, keeping them tucked away to contemplate before he faced the champion in future races.

After that, the two men were regular competitors. Owens usually beat Metcalfe in the 100-yard dash, but it was back and forth in the 220. When Owens started at Ohio State, the two competitors became close friends. Metcalfe, who was a junior at the time, looked after Owens, taking him under his wing both in personal matters and matters on the track.

Owens later wrote that Metcalfe was the greatest sprinter of the day (Owens 1972). Metcalfe was tall, powerful, and more muscular than Owens, and he had incredible willpower. Owens thought that the shorter races did a disservice to Metcalfe's abilities. At the time, African American runners were limited to the shorter distances: the 100- and 200-meter dashes, or the 100- and 220-yard dashes in the United States. Training for longer races involved access to tracks, and poor African American kids like Metcalfe and Owens had not had those resources. Instead, they had been limited to running on sidewalks and down school halls. Owens thought that allowing Metcalfe the opportunity to train for the longer races would have better realized his physical power. Owens remembered that in every 220 he raced against his friend, Metcalfe was ahead of him in those few yards after the finish line. Owens had the advantage of a quick start, where Metcalfe took a few seconds to get running. Once Metcalfe was underway, he was fast and would have been difficult to beat in a longer race.

These friendships and experiences sustained Owens throughout his life. The young men were teammates, and while they sometimes competed against one another on the track field, they stood by one another when the races were finished. Together they achieved incredible accomplishments, paving the way for other African American athletes who witnessed their victories. One of the most notable days was at the Big Ten finals in Ann Arbor, Michigan, on May 25, 1935. But Owens almost missed this major event.

THE BIG TEN FINALS

The Big Ten Conference was first established in 1896. It is a Division I intercollegiate conference that includes universities from Illinois, Indiana, Iowa, Michigan, Minnesota, Ohio, Pennsylvania, and Wisconsin. This was an important competition that the athletes trained for all year to win recognition for themselves and their schools.

Just a few days before the 1935 Big Ten finals in Ann Arbor, Michigan, Owens slipped and fell down some steps, hurting his back. On the day of the Big Ten meet, his condition was not improved. His friends had to lift him out of bed and into the rumble seat of the Model T they were driving. It seemed certain that Owens would not be able to compete that day. What would be the use of risking further injury and possibly jeopardizing his potential to compete in the future, particularly with the Olympic trials just a year away? Coach Snyder was reluctant to let him run.

Yet Owens was determined to work through his injury. He wanted to race. He had not come this far to sit on the sidelines. Owens told Snyder, "When you come from where I did, you don't really believe in tomorrows" (Owens 1972, 30). After much discussion, Snyder agreed to let Owens run the 100-yard dash, under the condition that he must stop immediately if there was any pain. He agreed.

As the meet was getting underway, trainers worked on Owens's back, massaging him and trying to loosen the pulled muscles. Once they finished, Owens did his usual warm-up routine. He jogged around 440-yard circuit, stretched for 10 minutes, did 5 minutes of practice starts (McRae 2002, 39). When his warm-ups ended, Owens was in a great deal of pain. He was not sure how he would continue, but his mentor Coach Riley was there to cheer him on. He had to try.

The first event was the 100-yard dash. Owens knew he had to get a good start. To do this, rather than waiting for the sound of the gun, he would watch the starter's eyes to anticipate when he would signal the start of the race (Owens 1972). This allowed Owens to take the lead immediately, and the strategy always seemed to work to his advantage. For this race he had a good start, a fast run, and he crossed the finish line first. The officials' timers were stopped at 9.31, 9.33, and 9.34 seconds (McRae 2002, 43). As was customary at that time, the final race time was rounded up to 9.4 seconds. Owens had tied the world record set by Frank Wykoff in 1930. Wykoff had set the record at an AAU track meet in Los Angeles, and although the record was not officially recognized by the international union until November of 1930 because of questions concerning the timing of such events, Wykoff had beat the former record holder Eddie Tolan by a full second. Wykoff's record, which he replicated again in June of 1930, stood for five years.

Seven minutes after his victory in the 100, Owens was standing in front of the long-jump pit. He had convinced Coach Snyder to let him continue with the event, telling the coach that his back was no longer hurting so much. Owens jumped 26 feet, 8¼ inches, breaking Nambu's world record by six inches. It was an incredible feat, but Owens did not have time to celebrate. Instead, he headed for the 220-yard final. Owens completed the race in 20.3 seconds, 10 yards ahead of the next competitor, and 0.3 second faster than the world record set in 1924. If his back was hurting now, he certainly did not notice it.

Owens had one event left. Less than an hour after he began his string of victories, Owens began the 220-yard low hurdle event. Owens finished out the afternoon leaping over 10 sets of wooden hurdles that were 2½ feet high and set 20 feet apart. Owens completed the race in 22.6 seconds, setting yet another record. In one short afternoon, with an aching back, Owens beat three world records and tied a fourth. No one had seen anything like it before.

The importance of Owens's accomplishments probably did not immediately set in for him, nor did the significance of the day. May 25, 1935 would forever be known as Jesse Owens's entry into the big leagues. His name and his accomplishments were noted in newspapers around the world, marking the beginning of his time as a celebrity athlete. Sports writer Joseph Sheehan wrote of Owens at the time: "It is a beautiful sight to watch Owens sprint. He runs as smoothly as but more gracefully than a well-oiled machine. He shows no apparent effort, so well-coordinated is his action. There is none of the visible exertion noticeable in other sprinters, as in Metcalfe, for instance, who fairly exudes power as he hurtles down the straightaway" (1935, 52). Owens raced in front of crowds that numbered in the tens of thousands, yet he remained modest and humble, always hoping to give his best effort at any event.

When the Big Ten meet was over, Owens returned to his parents' home at 2178 East 100th Street in Cleveland. Local reporter Alvin Silverman was there to do a story on Owens and his family for the *Cleveland Plain Dealer*. He reported on Owens's accomplishments at the meet, claiming that his was probably the "most extraordinary achievement in the history of organized track athletics, a history which dates to Ancient Greece" (McRae 2002, 56), but Silverman had not seen anything yet. Owens told him that he wanted to help the United States win the 1936 Olympics, and that he wanted to break every record in his events. Little did Silverman know how serious Owens was.

CALIFORNIA DREAMING

The next significant track meet after the Big Ten finals in 1935 involved traveling to Los Angeles for the NCAA track championships where the track meet would be held at the University of California–Berkeley for the very first time. It was a significant event in many ways, but perhaps most notably because it was the first time there were so many African American athletes competing in an intercollegiate event from primarily white universities (Fleming 1999).

By the time he made his way to the West Coast, Owens, who was now captain of the Ohio State team, had become quite a celebrity, and fans and autograph seekers mobbed around him at every turn. His name was as familiar among the American people as the name of the president of the United States, and members of the African American community began to look to Owens to conquer prejudice and racism as they watched him become successful within the context of traditionally racist social institutions (McRae 2002). Owens's enrollment at Ohio State, his accomplishments in athletics, and his coverage in the press began to excite the imaginations and hopes of African Americans who had long seen themselves as relegated to the segregated spaces outside of mainstream

American society. The expectation that Owens could begin to change this was no small matter. People saw Owens as a role model and a hero, and they hoped that he could do something to change the discrimination and suffering they faced. Yet Owens still struggled with racism and prejudice himself. He was starkly reminded of this when, in spite of his fame and accomplishments, he could not get a hotel room in downtown Los Angeles with fellow African American teammate Mel Walker (McRae 2002). Instead, the two teammates had to stay at the Sigma Chi Fraternity house at the University of Southern California campus. Owens did not write about how he felt when this happened, but given his response in other similar situations it is possible to imagine that he calmly accepted the events and made the best of his accommodations.

While in California, Owens was able to socialize and enjoy parties thrown in the athletes' honor. Owens was often the focus of much attention, and everywhere he went there were throngs of people trying to meet him. One of his most steadfast fans was a young 22-year-old socialite named Quincella Nickerson (McRae 2002). She was among the group of fans who had greeted Owens when he arrived at the train station in Los Angeles, and she was often seen in the stands at the field as the athletes worked out. Quincella's father, William Nickerson Jr., was president of the Golden Life Insurance Company and quite wealthy. Quincella, who was always well dressed and flirtatious, spent a great deal of time with Owens when he was in Los Angeles. The two would visit her father's office, have lunch or tea together, go shopping, or drive around in her powder-blue sedan. Owens invited Quincella to join him when he met celebrity well-wishers like Will Rogers, Mickey Rooney, Jack Oakie, Mae West, and Clark Gable. It was a very exciting time for Owens, and could cause any young person to feel proud and boastful. Yet Owens did not let the experience go to his head. Instead, the *Los Angeles Times* reported that he was "polite, calm, confident, and apparently not the least bit conceited. . . . Owens is very conscientious. . . . Owens wants to be a great athlete—and he expects to pay the price of living a reasonable life" (McRae 2002, 74).

On June 15, 1935, Owens won his quartet of events against the Southern California Trojans. Just a week later, on June 22, Owens again won each event, securing four national collegiate titles in the competition at Berkeley. Owens scored 40 of Ohio State's 41 points for the meet. This meant that Owens single-handedly scored more points than many other entire college teams competing that day, including Michigan, UCLA, Notre Dame, Princeton, Yale, Harvard, Stanford, and Temple (McRae 2002, 75).

On June 26, Owens entered a race in San Diego against his friend and rival from Temple University, Eulace Peacock. The formidable 6-feet-tall, 180-pound athlete was just a year younger than Owens. Peacock was also an Alabama native. The two shared a family legacy of slavery, experiences growing up in the North, and an ability to break track records. In fact, in 1933 Peacock set the junior world best in the long jump at a meet in New Jersey, a title he held for just two hours until Owens broke the record in Cleveland. In San Diego, the much-anticipated 100-yard race between these two competitors turned out to be a close one. Owens was declared the winner, but some who saw the race felt that Peacock beat Owens (McRae 2002).

Owens left California and headed to Lincoln, Nebraska, for the AAU National Championships, which opened on July second. Owens knew Peacock would be a serious challenge, as he was perhaps his biggest rival at the time. But Peacock was not the biggest problem on Owens's mind. On June 29, the *Pittsburgh Courier* carried a front-page story about Owens and Quincella, declaring that the two were engaged to be married. Ruth read the article. She was crushed. She had not heard from Owens since he had left for California, and it was hard for her to know what to think. She wrote him a 10-line letter, questioning him about the newspaper report, but he only needed to see the handwriting on the envelope to realize the pain he must have caused her (McRae 2002). Owens called Ruth as soon as he reached Lincoln, explaining that the newspaper story was wrong and that Quincella was only a friend. But it was too late. In spite of his claims to the press that he was planning to marry Ruth as soon as possible, the damage had been done. Owens wanted the track meet—his 18th since the Big Ten finals—to be over, so that he could return home to Cleveland to sort out his life with Ruth.

As the 100 yard got underway at the University of Nebraska Memorial Stadium, Owens lined up against Peacock and Metcalfe, an experienced runner and Olympic champion. Temperatures that day approached 102 degrees. It was a big race, and the runners were obviously nervous. After 11 false starts, the race finally was underway. Peacock won, followed by Metcalfe, and then Owens. After that, Peacock beat Owens by 3/4 inch in the long jump. In spite of the losses, Owens did not seem to mind. Instead, his thoughts were elsewhere. He was intent on Ruth, the only thing that mattered to him. He had caused her shame, and had to get home as soon as possible.

On July 5, 1935, Owens left Lincoln by train and headed to Cleveland. Four hours after returning home, he went to Ruth's house to marry her. The two were wed that same night. Owens had to convince the clerk of the Probate Court to issue the license at seven thirty p.m., while Ruth had to persuade the Reverend Ernest Hall of East Mount Zion Baptist Church to perform the ceremony at her parents' home (McRae 2002). Now Ruth's parents would no longer be able to keep them from seeing one another. The two realized their childhood dream. They would be together to raise their family, which already included little Gloria.

The next morning, Owens left Cleveland and his new bride for more track meets. Owens repeatedly ran against his rival Peacock, and again (and again) he lost. Peacock beat Owens in the 100 meter in Ontario, in Buffalo, and in New York. Peacock defeated Owens in 7 of the 10 100-meter dashes they ran against each other in 1935. People were beginning to talk about Peacock's potential in the Berlin Olympic Games, and they were downplaying Owens's ability to lead the field. Even Owens had begun to wonder if he could ever beat Peacock again. He told columnist Marvel Cooke of the *New York Amsterdam News*: "I've already reached my peak. Peacock is just now reaching his. He's a real athlete. I don't know whether I can defeat him again." (McRae 2002, 87).

Unfortunately, Owens would never even have the chance to try. After their last race, Peacock went on to compete in Milan, Italy, where he pulled a hamstring. He reinjured the muscle in the 1936 Penn Relays, dashing any hope he may have had to compete in the 1936 Olympics. The two rivals would not meet on the track again, but they would remain friends for a lifetime, bound by mutual respect for one another and their respective accomplishments.

During his collegiate career, Owens's accomplishments were impressive and some of his victories resulted in long-standing records that others could not defeat. He won eight individual NCAA championships in 1935 and 1936 for the short sprints, the low hurdles, and the long jump. His record for winning four titles in a single championship stood until 2006 when Xavier Carter, a sophomore at Louisiana State University, equaled that championship record in only one year. Yet the accomplishment was not exactly the same. A major difference was that Owens won his championships in individual competitions, while Carter's victories included running with a relay team. During his junior year alone, Owens competed in and won 42 events. Between 1935 and 1936, Owens also won six national AAU titles. He was clearly a force to be reckoned with on the track, but his toughest races were yet to come.

Jesse Owens, of East Technical High of Cleveland, Ohio, is shown in action in the 100-yard dash at the Interscholastic track meet in Chicago, Ill., June 17, 1933. Owens broke the record for the 220-yard dash with a time of 20.7 seconds; he ran the 100-yard dash in 9.4 seconds; and he leaped 24 feet, 9 and ¼ inches in the broad jump for a new prep record. (AP/WIDE WORLD PHOTOS)

Jesse Owens, of Ohio State University, crosses the finish line in the 220-yard dash with a record speed of 20.3 seconds at the Big Ten Western Conference Track and Field meet at the University of Michigan in Ann Arbor, Mich., May 25, 1935. Owens, nicknamed "Buckeye Bullet," broke three world records, and he tied the 100-yard dash record, 9.4 seconds. (AP/WIDE WORLD PHOTOS)

U.S. track and field stars, left to right: Cornelius Johnson, Jesse Owens, and Glenn Hardin. In the back row, left to right, are Marty Glickman, Gene Venzke, Albert J. Mangin, Foy Draper, and Forrest G. Towns. (AP/WIDE WORLD PHOTOS)

Olympic athlete Jesse Owens and his wife, Ruth, are surrounded by admirers after returning home to Cleveland, Ohio, from the Olympics on Aug. 25, 1936. Owens won four gold medals at the 11th Olympiad held in Berlin, Germany. (AP/WIDE WORLD PHOTOS)

Famed Olympic track and field star Jesse Owens shows youngsters at Boys Town in Marikina, near Manila, the mechanics of a good start while near the Philippines, December 11, 1955. Owens's tour was conducted under auspices of the U.S. Department of State. (AP/WIDE WORLD PHOTOS)

Chapter 4

THE 1936 OLYMPICS

When I came back to my native country, after all the stories about Hitler, I couldn't ride in the front of the bus. . . . I had to go to the back door. I couldn't live where I wanted. I wasn't invited to shake hands with Hitler, but I wasn't invited to the White House to shake hands with the President, either.

—*Owens, as quoted in Schwartz 2005*

The 1936 Olympic trials were held in New York City at Randall's Island Stadium in July of that same year. Jesse Owens traveled to the city with high hopes of realizing his dream of earning a spot on the U.S. Olympic team. Owens trained hard his entire career, but he had worked especially hard during the four years leading up to these trials. He wanted a chance to compete in the international forum, to run and jump against the best amateur athletes the world had to offer, and to prove himself a world-class athlete. Four years earlier, during the 1932 Olympic trials, Owens experienced a glimmer of what it might be like to compete on the international stage. Owens was set to race against Eddie Tolan, a talented and experienced runner who needed to secure his eyeglasses with tape when he raced. As luck would have it, Owens drew the best lane for the event, lane four, but he gave the lane to Tolan, who was suffering from a strained leg muscle. Owens realized that Tolan was the best chance for the Olympic team that year, and he knew that he was not quite ready for this level of competition (McRae 2002). Tolan beat Owens in the trials, and as Owens expected, he went on to win gold medals in the 100- and 200-meter races, just ahead of Owens's good friend Metcalfe, who won silver and bronze at the games. Tolan was called the fastest man in the world when the games concluded.

Now, four years later, Owens would not need to forfeit his luck. Instead, he would give the trials his all. He was ready to win, but he had competed enough to know that anything could happen—a bad start, an injury, or a misstep. It was all so precarious, no matter how hard someone worked or how talented he might be. Owens only needed to think about his injured friend Peacock to remind himself of this.

Yet Owens's luck held out, and his hard work and skill paid off. In the trials, he soundly won the 100-meter, 200-meter, and long-jump competitions to secure his position on the team. Other members of the 1936 Olympic track team included Owens's friends Dave Albritton and Ralph Metcalfe. There were 18 African Americans, including two women, on the U.S. Olympic team—three times the number of African Americans who had competed in the 1932 games (see Appendix 1 for a complete list).

As the trials concluded, the new Olympic athletes found themselves in the midst of much celebration and fanfare. Excitement was high as they anticipated the upcoming travel and competition in Germany. Many dignitaries and celebrities offered words of advice to the amateur athletes, including baseball great Babe Ruth. During a special dinner for the athletes, Ruth questioned Owens about whether he would win in Berlin. He was well aware of the young man's capabilities and he wanted to see Owens return home victorious. Owens humbly replied to the legendary athlete that he would certainly try. Ruth admonished him, stating "Tryin' don't mean shit. I don't try. I succeed." Then Ruth asked Owens yet again if he was going to win. Owens, quick to catch on to Ruth's lesson, said, "Sure I am" (McRae 2002, 193).

Owens would run yet again on the strength of his feet and the courage of his lungs against international competitors, some who held intense prejudices against African Americans, Jews, and other groups of people. Owens knew what he was facing, yet he yearned to compete at these games to demonstrate that the Nazis and those who agreed with them were wrong. Because of this, he spoke out against those who wished to boycott the games, even in the midst of the incredible international controversy about conditions in Nazi Germany.

STRUGGLES LEADING UP TO THE GAMES

The government in Germany evolved into a fascist dictatorship over the decades preceding the 1936 Olympic Games. The Weimar Republic was formed in Germany in 1919 after the Germans lost World War I, during a turbulent time when left- and right-wing factions struggled for power, and workers' strikes, hyperinflation, and other issues made the economy unstable. A decade later, when the stock market crashed, Germany spun into rapid economic decline. By 1932, there was high unemployment (20%) and those Germans who were fortunate enough to have jobs often did not work many hours. In this volatile context, political decision making became more centralized and emergency decrees were commonplace. In January of 1933, Adolph Hitler was sworn in as Chancellor, and the Nazi party assumed power.

During this period, sports became a highly valued aspect of German life and culture. After World War I, the Versailles Treaty limited military training in Germany, and athletics became a way to compensate for this as young Germans strengthened body and mind through physical activity. As the Nazis gained power, sports became a way to emphasize values like teamwork, physical fitness, and aggressive patriotism (Mandell 1987).

In 1931, the International Olympic Committee (IOC), led by the Belgian Count Henri de Baillet-Latour, awarded Berlin the games over Barcelona as a signal that the country had reentered the international community after its defeat in World War I. The committee did not know at the time that Hitler would become chancellor of Germany just two years later, nor could they have anticipated that he would turn the country into a fascist state. In 1933, freedoms of speech, assembly, and press were suspended; the first concentration camp was established at Dachau; and Jews, homosexuals, handicapped people, blacks, and Gypsies faced unimaginable atrocities. That same year, the German Boxing Federation announced that it would no longer allow Jews as fighters or referees, and the minister of education announced that Jews would not be able to participate in youth, welfare, or gymnastics organizations (Mandell 1987). In September of 1935, laws barring Jews from citizenship and limiting their rights had been issued at Nuremberg.

Countries around the world were aware of these conditions, and as early as 1933 questions were raised about the morality of the Nazi regime hosting the Olympic Games. By the time of the 1936 Olympic trials, there was a very real possibility that the United States and other countries, including Sweden, the Netherlands, and Czechoslovakia, would boycott the games. Some of the strongest arguments in support of boycotting the games occurred in the United States. Ernest Jahnke, an American whose father was a German immigrant, was expelled from the IOC because he urged athletes to boycott. As public outcry intensified, officials inspected German sports facilities. In 1934, Avery Brundage, president of the United States Olympic Committee (USOC), who replaced Jahnke on the IOC, was part of an inspection team who concluded that Jewish athletes were being treated fairly and that the games should proceed as planned. Further, Brundage felt that the games were about athletes, not politics.

In the end, Brundage convinced the AAU to send an American team to Berlin. The games would go on. Owens and his teammates were pleased with the decision. Owens, Peacock, and Metcalfe were among a group of athletes who wanted to compete, and they had written letters to Brundage encouraging the committee to proceed with the games. They argued that their victories would disprove Nazi theories on race.

In spite of the support of these high-profile athletes for the Olympic Games, there remained significant disagreement with Brundage's decision across the United States. Jeremiah Mahoney, president of the AAU, disagreed with Brundage and wanted to see the games stopped. Other American athletes felt the same way. Among the promising American athletes who decided to boycott the Olympic trials in opposition to Nazi anti-Semitism were Herman Neugass, a Jewish sprinter from Tulane University, Harvard track teammates Milton Green and Norman Cahners, and the predominantly Jewish Long Island University basketball team.

Some athletes who boycotted the games created a counter-Olympics called the World Labor Athletics Carnival, which was held in August 1936 on Randall Island, New York. Sponsored by the AAU, the American Federation of Labor (AFL), and the Jewish Labor Committee, the event had several dignitaries who served as honorary chairs: New York Governor Herbert Lehman, New York City Mayor Fiorello LaGuardia, AFL President William Green, and Judge Jeremiah Mahoney, the former AAU president and leader of the Move the Olympics movement. Isidore Nagler, vice president of the International Ladies' Garment Workers' Union, chaired the labor committee for the event. On August 15 and 16, over 400 athletes from the United States participated in the counter-Olympic games, including teams that represented local New York labor unions. The event had widespread press coverage, and it was held again in 1937 to continue the protest of Nazi atrocities.

These activities did not dampen the spirits of international and U.S. athletes set to compete in Berlin. In August of 1936, Germany was ready to receive the international athletes and the world. The country had been scrubbed clean to hide anti-Jewish slogans and the public persecution of Jews. Yet it could not be hidden that there was not a single Jew on the German Olympic team. Hitler would make no apologies for this. He fully expected that Aryan supremacy would be proved through the Olympic Games, and he did not attempt to conceal his views. Joseph

Goebbels, Hitler's minister of propaganda, explained the importance of athletics in Nazi Germany on April 23, 1933: "German sport has only one task: to strengthen the character of the German people, imbuing it with the fighting spirit and steadfast camaraderie necessary in the struggle for its existence" (United States Holocaust Memorial Museum).

Goebbels convinced Hitler that the games would be an important propaganda event for the country, even though Hitler, an extreme nationalist, was wary of the international attention the games would bring. Hans von Tschammer und Osten, who was close to Hitler and head of the Reich Sports Office, oversaw the German Olympic Committee's planning for the 1936 games.

OWENS EN ROUTE TO GERMANY: THE *SS MANHATTAN*

On July 15, 1936, just three days after the Olympic trials in New York City ended, Jesse Owens boarded the *SS Manhattan* in his only suit, a blue pinstripe, with $7.90 in his pocket (Owens 1970). Cabin 87 on Deck D, below the water line, would be Owens's quarters for nine days as he sailed across the Atlantic Ocean from New York to Hamburg, Germany. The ship, a 24-ton luxury liner, was named after the New York City borough. Built by the New York Shipbuilding Company and launched just five years earlier, the liner carried 1,064 passengers to Hamburg, including 334 of the 382 Olympic athletes and 50 Olympic officials. An Olympic flag flew high above the ship, raised to the top of the mast during a ceremony as the ship got underway (*New York Times* 1936).

It did not take long for Owens's life on the boat to fall into a comfortable routine. He exercised on the ship's deck each morning, rested in the afternoon, and socialized with the other athletes on the boat in the evening. Even though the track athletes were advised not to run on the ship because the trainers felt it would contribute to shin splints, he jogged on the sun deck as part of his workout routine (Daley 1936). He also did some calisthenics. Owens kept a journal to record his experiences, and he wrote letters to Ruth each day. Although he kept busy, the trip to Berlin was filled with anticipation. Uniforms were distributed aboard the ship, and the excitement was palpable. Owens tried patiently to await his arrival in Germany, eager to prove himself in the Berlin stadium.

Coaches of notable athletes were permitted to accompany them on the ship on the trip to Berlin. Among these coaches was Larry Snyder, who had several track athletes from Ohio State on the Olympic team. One of his responsibilities en route to the games was to find two more pairs of kangaroo-hide track shoes for Owens. Souvenir hunters had already stolen two pairs, and Owens was supposed to arrive at the games equipped with three pairs of shoes (Mandell 1987).

Owens enjoyed getting to know his teammates as the group made their way to Berlin. Some of the athletes were seasick, and 400-meter champion Harold Smallwood had appendicitis en route to Berlin, but most stayed very focused on the games to come. One exception was Olympic swimmer Eleanor Holm Jarrett of Brooklyn, who was not quite as self-disciplined aboard the ship as Owens and some of the other athletes. Jarrett reportedly trained on cigarettes and champagne. The statuesque beauty had a wild time on the way to Berlin, enjoying raucous parties each evening. Her behavior caught the attention of the women chaperones and other officials on the ship, and she received warnings for her behavior. Finally, on the last evening on the ship, after failing to heed a warning from Avery Brundage, she was dismissed from the team. Jarrett's athletic career ended, and she later watched from the stands as the Olympic gold for her best event, the 100-meter backstroke, went to the Dutch swimmer Nida Senff.

The SS Manhattan arrived in the Hamburg harbor on July 23, 1936. Always likeable, Owens was winning contests before he even disembarked from the ship. While on board, Owens was voted the best dressed man (McRae 2002), in spite of the four-year-old suit he thought did not fit well (Owens 1970), and he was also voted the second-most popular teammate after middle-distance runner Glenn Cunningham (Mandell 1987).

The team traveled from Hamburg to Berlin by train, and then by bus to the city hall for a reception. It was here that Owens first heard the Germans chanting his name, "Yes-say Oh-vens," over and over again. His fame preceded him across the Atlantic, and Germany was anticipating Owens's arrival. Autograph seekers were in constant pursuit of the world-famous athlete. German newspapers recounted stories of his athletic feats, and one German paper, keeping true to Nazi racist propaganda, even printed pictures of Owens beside those of apes, suggesting that his athletic abilities were due to animal-like qualities. Owens knew it was all myth. Just a year earlier, Coach Snyder arranged for Howard University professor William Montague Cobb to examine Owens's body to see if there was any truth to claims that African Americans' athletic abilities were related to racial characteristics. He measured Owens's arms and legs, did x-rays to examine his bone structure, and determined that there was nothing unique about Owens's body. Instead, his athletic prowess was due to "industry, training, incentive and courage" when he prepared for and competed in his sporting events (McRae 2002, 93).

THE OLYMPIC VILLAGE

Representing 49 countries, 3,963 athletes from around the world competed in the 1936 Olympic events. This number included 331 women. Germany had the largest team with 348 athletes, and the United States had the second largest with 312 competitors. All the male athletes lived together in the Olympic Village designed by Wolfgang Fuerstner, who acted as the head of the village. Fuerstner worked hard to see his vision for the village become reality, and indeed it set standards worldwide for athletic accommodations. Yet in spite of his accomplishments and contributions, when Fuerstner's partly Jewish heritage was discovered, he was stripped of his German citizenship. Sadly, he committed suicide just two days after the Olympic Games ended.

The Olympic lodging was beautifully situated in the middle of a forest of birch trees, complete with a lake and snow-white ducks. The village was like a small city. There were 160 housing units for the male athletes alone, with each house accommodating 24–26 athletes. The athletes stayed in double rooms, and each double room had its own bathroom. There were common rooms where athletes could meet to play cards, watch films, and visit. The village had its own hospital, library, theater, restaurant, swimming pool, dentist, and barbershop. Each team had its own steward who was fluent in the team's home language, and each had its own chef to prepare foods from their home cuisine. Owens would eat well during his stay in the Olympic village; he could enjoy steaks, bacon, eggs, ham, and other popular American foods. Busses would transport the athletes to and from the stadium. This could be inconvenient, depending on the bus schedule and the timing of the athletes' events.

Women athletes were treated worse than the men. They stayed in the Friedrich Friesen Haus, a dormitory near the Reichssportfeld (the Olympic stadium) that was surrounded by a large wrought-iron fence. The women were isolated and kept under strict supervision. Sometimes there was no heat in the building, and food was limited in quantity and quality. Complaints from women athletes went largely unheeded (Mandell 1987).

While staying at the Olympic village, Owens met many famous athletes, including the fighter Max Schmeling. The boxer had just returned to Germany from New York where he defeated Joe Louis, Owens's good friend, in a much-publicized fight. Schmeling was hailed a German hero, and he was instrumental in helping to convince the U.S. Olympic Committee not to boycott the Berlin games. Schmeling later admitted that this was extremely naïve on his part, although he was not totally naïve about the Nazi party and Hitler's campaign. Schmeling resisted pressure to join the Nazi party, and he retained Joe Jacobs, his American manager, who was Jewish.

OPENING CEREMONIES

The Olympic games opened amid unprecedented fanfare on August 1, 1936 with Hitler, Goring, and Goebbels presiding over the events. During the opening ceremonies it was immediately obvious that these games would be more lavish than any the world had seen before. Dramatic musical fanfares by German composer Richard Strauss alerted the crowd that Hitler and other party officials had arrived. As the Führer walked into the stadium, Strauss led his orchestra in *Deutschland über Alles*. Once the crowd saw Hitler, they broke into chants of "Sieg Heil!"

Once the dignitaries were seated, the athletic teams, arranged in alphabetic order, entered the stadium. Many teams gave a Nazi salute to the box where the officials sat. The Italians, Turks, Austrians, and Bulgarians offered the full-arm salute. The British offered Eyes Right in deference to the German hosts and dignitaries. The French offered what appeared to be a Nazi salute, although some later claimed that it was simply an Olympic salute (Mandell 1987). When the Americans entered the stadium, led by Avery Brundage and gymnastics champion Alfred Joachim, the athletes only removed their straw hats and placed them over their chests. They did not dip the flag. This tradition of not dipping the American flag to any "earthly king" was established during the 1908 Olympic Games in London (Mandell 1987, 150). At these games, the British did not fly an American flag in the stadium, and so the American athletes carried their own banner, refusing to dip it when they passed the British monarchy.

More than 110,000 people attended the opening ceremonies. The boys from the Hitler Youth released 20,000 white doves. This was followed by a 21-gun salute signaling a sole runner to ignite the Olympic torch to begin the games. Over 335 runners had carried the Olympic torch to the stadium, each traveling one kilometer of the total distance from Peloponnesus, in Greece, to Berlin (Mandell 1987). This was the first time the Olympic flame was carried to the modern games in this manner.

After the Olympic torch was lit, the athletes recited the Olympic oath, led by German weight lifter Rudolf Ismayr. As they finished, the orchestra and chorus began to perform the "Hallelujah Chorus" from Handel's *Messiah*. When they concluded, Spiridon Louis, the Greek shepherd who became a national hero during the 1896 Olympics as the first man to win the marathon, emerged from the midst of the Greek athletes. He humbly offered a wild sprig from Mount Olympus, the site of the first Olympics, to the Führer. As he presented it, he said: "I present to you this olive branch as a symbol of love and peace. We hope that the nations will ever meet solely in such peaceful competition" (Mandell 1987, 153). The orchestra and chorus continued with the "Hallelujah Chorus," and emotions ran high among the spectators.

The opening ceremonies concluded with an evening presentation of the Pageant of Youth. Over 10,000 German boys and girls performed for the crowd, followed by ballet dancers. The night ended with a stunning choral performance of Beethoven's Ninth Symphony, including the famous "Ode to Joy," with words penned by the German poet Friedrich Schiller.

This was clearly an event to remember, filled with pageantry, drama, and symbolism. German citizens could view some of the events televised to 21 different centers, while Americans and others around the world learned of the events through radio and newspaper reports. Photographs of the events could only be obtained from the German press so that images of Germany could be protected during the games. So that the moment would not be lost, the IOC and the German Ministry of Propaganda commissioned Leni Riefenstahl, the famous German filmmaker, to direct the entire filming of the 1936 Olympics. Riefenstahl, a former dancer and actress, had captured Hitler's attention and trust when she filmed the 1933 short film *Der Sieg des Glaubens (The Victory of Faith)*, which captured the Nazi party rally at Nuremberg. She followed this with the 1934 film *Triumph des Willens (Triumph of the Will)*, an account of the 1934 Nuremberg rally. With unlimited resources available to her, Riefenstahl produced the award-winning and controversial film later considered to be one of the most effective propaganda pieces ever created.

At the time of the 1936 Olympics, Riefenstahl had qualified to be a member of the German cross-country skiing team. Rather than compete in the events, however, she decided instead to create a film of the games, which she later called *Olympia*. Several technical innovations were incorporated into the film. Riefenstahl had her crew, which included 30 cameramen, dig pits so that cameramen could film pole-vaulters and other athletes with the sky and the Olympic flame in the background, and she used balloons with small cameras to get aerial views of the events. Special camera lenses were created and used to get close-ups of athletes' faces, and some of the most famous footage includes coverage of Jesse Owens lining up with other athletes before the 100-meter race, appearing very calm and at ease. In the film, Riefenstahl devoted more attention to Owens than any other individual competitor at these events (Mandell 1987).

At the games, Riefenstahl set new standards for filming sporting events. Some parts of the movie were shot during training, and then spliced into the actual footage to add to the dramatic impact of the film. Riefenstahl added music to convey meaning about the athletes' efforts, trials, and victories. She created tracks for the cameras so that she could get footage of athletes in motion and the crowd's responses. She used underwater shooting during high-diving events so that athletes could be seen as they swam to the surface after their dive, and rafts were pulled alongside the swimmers to get close up shots of their faces.

Riefenstahl, who was criticized for creating Nazi propaganda, later claimed that Hitler was not pleased with the film. She explained that he was not interested in the Olympics and did not like the games. According to Riefenstahl, Hitler did not like the stadium and the architecture, and he did not enjoy seeing African Americans win. She claimed that it took a lot of convincing to get Hitler to the games (*The Wonderful, Horrible Life of Leni Riefenstahl* 1993).

Overall, it took Riefenstahl two years to edit the film. There was more than 400,000 meters of film to review, and watching it alone took over 10 weeks. Riefenstahl treated the project as a dramatic film. She opened with an actor who played the role of an ancient Greek participating in the original games. She decided to use music to help show the willpower of the athletes, and she used angles that dramatized the events.

Riefenstahl's work was highly controversial, and film showings that included *Olympia* were often accompanied by protestors. Riefenstahl visited the United States in 1938, where she received mixed American reactions to her presence and the film. The English-language version of *Olympia* was first shown in Avery Brundage's home to about 100 people, and she was kindly greeted by Henry Ford in Chicago and Walt Disney in Florida. Yet newspapers across the country ran ads by the Anti-Nazi League calling for boycotts against her, and Hollywood gave her the cold shoulder. The film was set to be shown in Radio City Music Hall, but the viewing was abruptly cancelled and the manager fired, which in her memoir Riefenstahl attributed in part to the "terrible events of Kristallnacht" (1992, 239), the Night of Broken glass, which occurred as she was en route to the United States. During Kristallnacht, thousands of Jewish homes and shops were ransacked, and shattered glass from broken windows covered the street. Jews were beaten to death, synagogues were burned, and over 30,000 Jewish men were taken to concentration camps. While Riefenstahl claimed that Disney wanted to see her film, he refused, perhaps fearing the repercussions if the public found out, and he later claimed that when he met her he was unaware of who she was.

Around the world, Riefenstahl was accused of expressing a fascist spirit through the film as she celebrated the body beautiful, physical strength, and athletic perfection. Later, when questioned about this, Riefenstahl claimed that art and politics were two different things, and that her work was art. She explained that one had nothing to do with the other (*The Wonderful, Horrible Life of Leni Riefenstahl* 1993). During the war, she continued to shoot dramatic films, using Gypsies being held in concentration camps as extras. She later explained that she knew nothing of what was going on in Hitler's Germany, and she was never persecuted for crimes because there was not enough evidence to convict her.

THE GAMES BEGIN

After the opening ceremonies ended, the qualifying heats for the various events began. The first qualifying heat for Owens was the 100-meter race, held on Sunday, August 2. Just a month before this race, Owens did not even know if he would qualify for the Olympic games. Now here he was set to compete in the chance of a lifetime. Owens rode the bus from the village to the stadium early in the morning, cramped among the other athletes who patted him on the back and cheered for their famous teammate (Mandell 1987). Owens wore his gray team sweat suit over the white Olympic uniform to help him keep warm in the Berlin dampness and rain. The number 723 was pinned to his chest, identifying him to officials from around the world. Owens donned track shoes made by 69 *Gebrüder Dassler Schuhfabrik*, a German firm that later split into two companies, Adidas and Puma.

Once he arrived at the Berlin stadium, Owens became reacquainted with German sprinter Erich Borchmeyer, a competitor he beat in a race in Los Angeles in 1932. Only the top two runners in the qualifying heat would make it into the quarterfinals. In his opening run, Owens tied the world record at 10.3 seconds. As if this were not enough, in his quarterfinal match, Owens beat the world record by 0.1 second, finishing the race in 10.2 seconds. Later, it was determined that this was a wind-assisted record, and it was ruled inadmissible (McRae 2002).

The next event Owens faced was the qualifying heat for the broad jump. Owens was in competition with a popular and competitive German athlete, Luz Long. Long had already set an Olympic record during the preliminary round of the event. Yet while Long was setting records, Owens was struggling. He fouled in his first two attempts to advance in the competition. When Long noticed his competitor's struggle, he advised Owens to jump six inches before the takeoff board so that he would not foul again. Long knew that Owens would be able to propel himself far enough, even with this six-inch loss, to qualify for the finals. Long was the consummate athlete, even searching for the toughest competition in the event of his life. With Long's advice in mind Owens did qualify for the event, and the two faced each other in the finals.

After this, Owens and Long became fast friends in spite of their language and cultural differences. Long spoke some English, but Owens knew no German. In spite of this, the two shared stories of their families and hopes. Each man was married and had a small child at home. They talked at length about religion, and the German views on race. Long did not believe the Nazi propaganda. Instead, he treated his new friend as an equal, learning about his life and respecting him as an individual and accomplished athlete. Owens later wrote that Long was the best friend he ever had (Owens 1978).

The 100-meter dash was the first final event for Owens at the Berlin Olympics. The competition was stiff. Three of the men who had competed to be in the final race held world records for the event at 10.3 seconds: Ralph Metcalfe, Jesse Owens, and Christian Berger of Holland (Mandell 1987). After he dug toe holes in the track to start the race, Owens lined up against Metcalfe and Wykoff from the U.S., Strandberg from Sweden, Borchmeyer from Germany, and Osendarp from Holland. In the final heat, Owens won, and clocked a world record 10.2 seconds. The record was later disallowed when German officials determined there was a following wind that may have contributed to Owens's victory. Metcalfe took silver behind his teammate after stumbling at the start of the race (Mandell 1987). Osendarp took bronze.

During the awards ceremony, a laurel wreath was placed on Owens's head as he stood on the winner's dais. A German woman placed the gold medal around his neck and gave him a small potted oak from the Black Forest as the orchestra played "The Star-Spangled Banner." It was certainly one of the most memorable moments in Owens's life, and one that would forever change him.

Although Hitler was in attendance at the games when Owens won, he showed no acknowledgement toward Owens after his victory. While Hitler initially greeted many of the medalists in his box, including the first Germans to win gold medals (Tilly Fleischer for women's javelin, and Hans Woelke for men's shot put), he abruptly left the box before Cornelius Johnson and Dave Albritton, both African Americans, won gold and silver medals in the high jump. Some claim that Hitler left because the event stretched late into the evening and the weather was poor and threatening rain (Mandell 1987). Others believed the chancellor left the stadium because of his racist perspective and his unwillingness to greet African American winners. Later, Nazi officials claimed that they suggested to Hitler that he should either greet all or none of the winners, and he decided to greet none of them. Whatever the cause of his absence, the press picked up on this. Headlines across the United States noted Hitler's racist attitudes and his snubbing of African American Olympic winners, particularly Owens, and this became part of the lore surrounding Owens's participation in the games.

On August 4—day three of the Olympic games—Owens ran qualifying heats for the 200-meter race and competed in the long jump. In the 200 meter, Owens broke the world record, running the event in 21.2 seconds, a time he would repeat in the second qualifying heat. Then he went to the long-jump area. The final for the running broad jump was against Long. On his final jump, Long tied Owens and set a new European record. But the competition was not over. Owens would have the last jump. Unbelievably, Owens's final jump set a new Olympic record, measuring 26 feet, 5 inches, and he won the gold medal for the event, overcoming his earlier struggles to even qualify for this competition. Long was the first to congratulate Owens as the two waited for the medals ceremony to begin. Years later, Long was posthumously awarded the Pierre de Coubertin medal for sportsmanship, given by the International Olympic Committee to recognize athletes who exhibit sportsmanship during the games, in honor of the founder of the modern Olympics.

The day after winning gold in the long jump, Owens faced the 200-meter finals. In Berlin, the race was on a curved track, not the typical straightaway Owens typically raced on during competitions. Owens would run on an unusually cold and rainy day in Berlin against teammate Matthew "Mack" Robinson, who won the qualifying heat. Robinson was the older brother of Jackie Robinson, who later broke the color barrier and earned fame on the baseball field. Mack Robinson was one of the few runners to ever beat Owens. Owens also faced Osendarp of Holland, who had come in third behind Owens and Metcalfe in the 100-meter race, Haenni of Switzerland, Orr from Canada, and van Bevern of Holland. In the finals, Owens had a strong start and pulled ahead of his competitors, winning the finals with a record-breaking 20.7 seconds. Robinson came in second place, securing the silver at 21.1, and Osendarp came in third, clocking in at 21.3.

Jesse Owens's final event in the 1936 Olympics came on August 9, 1936. This event was not something Owens anticipated as he traveled to Berlin, even though it was an event the U.S. team had typically won. The United States had traditionally done well in the 4 × 100-meter relay race, winning the event in every Olympic game up to that point since 1920 (Mandell 1987). The 1936 relay team originally included Sam Stoller and Marty Glickman, the only Jews on the U.S. team, along with Ralph Metcalfe and Frank Wykoff. Stoller and Glickman were competing well in Berlin, and the two had come in first and second place in the trial race run earlier in the week (McRae 2002). Yet in spite of their successes, American coaches Lawson Robertson and Dean Cromwell, likely under pressure from Avery Brundage, decided that Owens and Foy Draper should run in their place for the relay final. Controversy ensued as people questioned whether the decision was driven by acquiescence to the Nazis. Even though Owens stood up for the Jewish members of the team, nothing changed. Instead, he was warned to do as he was told. Argentina, Italy, Germany, Canada, and Holland all had tough teams competing in the relay, and the American coaches wanted to win.

When the race began, Owens ran the first leg, and then he passed the baton off to Metcalfe. Metcalfe passed to Draper, and Wykoff finished the race. The American team won the race and set a new world record at 39.8 seconds, primarily because of Owens's strong lead in the event (Mandell 1987). The Italian team came in second place after the Americans, and the Germans secured the bronze. Typical of his generous nature, Owens insisted that Metcalfe stand on the podium for the team since he had been in two Olympics, but never won the gold. His gesture did not conceal the fact that Owens was the first athlete in Olympic history to win four gold medals.

In the end, the U.S. Olympic athletes fared well in the Berlin games. African American athletes won 14 medals, one-fourth of the 56 medals American athletes brought home from the games. This is a remarkable accomplishment given that they constituted just over 5 percent of the total team membership. The only team to beat the Americans in the final medal count was Germany, whose athletes won 89 total medals.

THE POST-GAMES OLYMPIC TOUR

The Olympic games concluded on August 16, 1936. After the closing ceremonies, Owens set off on a European exhibition tour with his teammates on the track team. U.S. Coaches Robinson and Cromwell insisted that the team go on the tour. They traveled first to Cologne, Germany, where organizers promised the AAU that they would increase the percentage of ticket-sale proceeds to the organization from 10 to 15 if Owens raced (McRae 2002). In spite of his exhaustion, Owens raced Metcalfe in the 100 meter. Owens felt good that day, and he had a quick start in the race. He even thought he might beat his own world record. Then he heard Metcalfe's pounding stride behind him. As he crossed the finish line the world record was tied, but it was Metcalfe who won the race. Owens congratulated Metcalfe, deeply admiring the integrity of this man who cared so much and drove himself even in exhibition games (Owens 1972). When the games concluded for the day, the team was expected to attend a banquet that lasted until midnight. There would be no rest for the tired athletes.

After Cologne, the team left immediately for more competitions in Prague, and then they returned to Germany to a town called Bochum before proceeding on to London. Owens did not want to go. He was physically drained from his Olympic experience, and he had lost 12 pounds. Yet AAU President Brundage and his deputy, Daniel Ferris, insisted. The fee for the American team to enter the Olympics was $350,000, and when the team set sail for Germany, they were still short on funds. The exhibition games were a way for the athletes to earn money for the American team to meet its financial obligations. The track and field team earned money for the Olympic committee at every event in the exhibitions, provided Owens ran the sprints and jumped. Crowds paid money to see the famous athlete compete. The exhibitions were an effort to clear $30,000 in debt the organization held when the games began. By the time the exhibition tour ended, Brundage was able to cover the fees and pay an additional $50,000 to the American Olympic Association (Mandell 1987).

As Owens embarked on the tour, words of congratulations and lucrative job offers began to pour in from across the United States. Rumors abounded about the significant money Owens would make when he returned, and many of the telegraphs he received suggested that job offers and other deals were waiting for him when he returned home. One rumor was that Eddie Cantor, a radio comedian, would pay Owens $40,000 for a 10-week engagement (Mandell 1987). This was an extraordinary amount of money in 1936—more than Owens ever could have imagined earning.

In spite of his fame and the rumors of impending wealth, Owens had no money as he traveled, and the conditions were sometimes difficult as he was jostled from one place to the next. In Prague, a fellow passenger bought him a sandwich and some milk. In Croydon Airport outside of London, Owens and Coach Snyder slept on mattresses in an empty hangar at the airport (McRae 2002). Owens was weary and suspicious of the continued demands on the athletes. At one point, Owens told the *New York Times*, "Somebody's making money somewhere . . . they are trying to grab everything they can and we can't even buy a souvenir of the trip" (McRae 2002, 165).

Adding to his misery, Owens was losing races. He lost in his first races in Cologne, and he continued to lose in subsequent meets. Feeling as though he had tarnished his gold medals, he became gloomy. Owens liked to win, to please the crowd, and he did not want to run under these conditions and with these results. He had already trained for more than a year, and he ran harder than ever before during the Olympic competition. Now he was tired and he wanted to go home (Owens 1970). Rather than go on to Stockholm, Sweden, and the Scandinavian leg of the tour with the rest of his team, Owens made a monumental decision. He would leave. Owens sent a telegram to the AAU to inform them of his decision:

SICK AND UNDERWEIGHT. CANNOT COMPETE IN STOCKHOLM. FAMILY WAITING FOR ME. GOING HOME. JESSE OWENS. (Owens 1970, 163)

Rather than offering to assist Owens in finding a job or some money to help with his travels or giving him time to rest a bit before continuing to compete, the AAU expelled him from amateur competition, claiming breach of contract. Owens's decision to withdraw from the post-Olympic exhibitions resulted in him being barred from future Olympic competition as well as any college or amateur competition. Owens would never again race against other athletes in a track and field competition, even though he had never been paid to compete in track events. Up to that point, he had earned no money for his athleticism. Owens felt used and betrayed. All of his hard work and talent, including the attention and glory he brought to the United States and his team, would not be enough to allow him to compete again.

Owens was not the first Olympic athlete to become embroiled in decisions about amateur competitions. Longstanding debates over amateurism are part of Olympic history. Avery Brundage was a central figure in these early debates. Brundage competed in the 1912 Olympics in Stockholm, placing sixth in the decathlon, the same event Jim Thorpe won. Thorpe later was stripped of his gold medals for the decathlon and pentathlon when officials learned that he had played two seasons of amateur baseball before competing in the Olympic games. Brundage did not support restoring Olympic medals to Thorpe; instead, Brundage sought to uphold strict rules on amateurism. He believed that athletes who were amateurs competed purely out of love for the sport, and no athlete should be paid to compete in an athletic event. If an athlete received money, he or she was no longer an amateur. These same strict rules would impact Owens's career for the rest of his life.

GOING HOME

Jesse Owens, the world-famous athlete, returned home on the SS *Queen Mary*. He returned victorious, a celebrated hero who had won a record four gold medals. People around the world knew his name and his accomplishments. He was certainly the most famous and admired African American athlete in the world. His face was on newspapers around the world, and he was about to be greeted by the New York elite.

Yet all was not well, nor would it be for a long time. Owens had survived the racial tensions in Germany only to face yet more racism in the United States. First he heard of his parents' struggles when they arrived in New York City. Henry and Emma Owens, who had taken the train from Cleveland to New York to greet their son at his homecoming, were unable to find a hotel that would allow them to stay the night. After being refused a room at four places, the parents of the most famous athlete in the world finally were permitted to check into the Hotel Pennsylvania (McRae 2002).

Later, Owens faced his own difficulties as he struggled to find a way to earn money in the aftermath of the Olympics. When he arrived home, Owens was greeted with job offers, movie offers, and parades, including a ticker-tape parade in New York City. After he entered New York harbor aboard the *Queen Mary* on August 24, 1936, reuniting with his family and friends, celebrations abounded. He was wined and dined and promised lucrative jobs. Bill "Bojangles" Robinson, the famous African American entertainer and tap dancer who was one of the first to greet Owens, helped to arrange for Marty Forkins to be Owens's agent. Forkins, who was Robinson's lifelong manager, predicted that he could pull together deals that would bring in $100,000 (McRae 2002, 172).

To Owens's dismay, none of these promises panned out. He took tap-dancing lessons from Bojangles, hoping to at least find work as a nightclub performer while Coach Snyder attempted to get a reprieve of the AAU ban for Owens so that he could run track again. Owens also appealed to the Cleveland branch of the AAU, making the case that he was never paid to run track. This was to no avail. The final blow came at the end of 1936 when the AAU gave Glenn Morris, who won the decathlon in Berlin, the AAU's Sullivan Trophy, which was awarded annually to the best track and field athlete of the year. Two weeks before this, Owens had been voted America's sportsman of the year by an Associated Press landslide vote, but the AAU saw things differently. While Owens laughed off the slight in public, Marty Forkins fumed. He accused Ferris, Brundage's deputy at the AAU, of persecuting Owens ever since the Berlin Olympics (McRae 2002).

On September 3, the Olympic track team returned to the United States. Owens reunited with his teammates for a huge parade in New York City. Thousands of people came to cheer for the team and to get a look at the famous Jesse Owens. Yet Owens and other African Americans were crowded into two cars, a gesture the *Chicago Defender* referred to as being "Jim Crowed in the parade of honor" (McRae 2002, xx). When word reached Harlem about this treatment of the athletes, residents expressed their displeasure. The few who remained to see the parade hissed at the procession, and some, including young children, chanted "Jesse Owens Jim Crowed" over and over again (172).

By year's end, Owens finally conceded that he would not be able to run competitively again as an amateur. He needed to earn money to support his family, and he wanted to return to Ohio State to finish his education. With these goals in front of him, Owens allowed Forkins to set up some deals so that he could make money.

While no one spoke openly of it, Owens and his family began to wonder if he really had broken out from the legacy of slavery and racism, and whether the American dream could possibly come true for a poor black boy from rural Alabama. Henry Owens was not to be fooled. He told his son, "J. C., it don't do a colored man no good to get himself too high. Cause it's a helluva drop back to the bottom" (Owens 1970, 39). Little did Owens know how soon that drop would come, and how far he would fall.

Chapter 5

TENUOUS CIRCUMSTANCES

I've been a Negro in America . . . and I want to tell you it can be pure hell at times.

—*Owens 1970, 17*

After the Olympics, Jesse Owens realized that he would probably never again compete on the amateur circuit. He considered returning to Ohio State, but he could not afford to pay the tuition and costs. His brother Sylvester offered to help with college expenses, but Owens would not accept. In all honesty, he thought that Sylvester had already sacrificed too much for him, that Sylvester instead was the one who should be going to college (Owens 1970). Sylvester was always the smart one, but he had not had the opportunity to finish high school because he had to work to contribute to the family's earnings.

The weeks after the Olympics were difficult and trying for Owens. He had been on top of the world as the Olympic champion, and now within a matter of days he was plummeting to the depths of despair. Not only was he was no longer able to run competitively, but he could not return to school, and no one offered him a job, even though many had promised to do so after he won Olympic gold. The best option for him was to return home to be with his family.

Owens was not a selfish man, and he never sought great riches for himself. Instead, he spent his money on those he cared about, and sometimes on acquaintances and strangers who just asked him for help. In the months after the Olympics, Owens was able to purchase a $6,000 house for his parents in Cleveland. The house had 11 rooms—enough for the family, which continued to grow as the Owens children married and had children of their own. He spent $2,000 on furniture for the new home. Owens bought a new Buick for himself, and he made a down payment on a new car for his former coach Charles Riley (McRae 2002). But soon his money had run out, and he faced even more difficult decisions.

Owens spent the next years of his life struggling to make an honest living in a country that both loved and despised him. People loved him for his athletic accomplishments and good will, but generally the nation was not able to reconcile his accomplishments with the racist attitudes and institutions prevalent in the United States at the time. With a young and growing family, Owens hoped for steady work and enough money to make ends meet, but he could not have both. He needed to travel and deliver speeches, which meant being away from home, in order to provide for his family in a way he thought was acceptable. The 1940s and 1950s proved to be uneven and trying times for Owens as he found himself in the public eye, but under tenuous circumstances.

NEGRO BASEBALL LEAGUE AND SELF-PROMOTION

After the Olympics, Owens's business manager Marty Forkins secured some endorsement deals for Owens with some African American companies, and Forkins also arranged for him to appear at ball games and other social functions to maintain his public presence. After Owens returned to Cleveland, promoters from the Negro baseball league approached him, asking for help with the game (Owens 1972). The league was created for talented and skilled ballplayers who were not able to play in the major leagues because of their race. African American players were denied the chance to play baseball on integrated teams beginning in 1868 when the National Association of Base Ball Players (NABBP), the first professional sports league, ruled unanimously that it would bar "any club which may be composed of one or more colored persons" (see Riley 1983 for a history of the league).

Only a few African American baseball players participated in professional baseball leagues around this time. One notable African American ballplayer was Moses Fleetwood "Fleet" Walker, a catcher for the Northwestern League's Toledo Blue Stockings beginning in 1883. At the time, Toledo was a minor league team, but in 1884, it joined the American Association, making it a professional league. Walker's brother Welday also played in six games for Toledo. These men suffered intense discrimination from racist baseball players like first baseman Cap Anson, who refused to play if Walker was on the other team, and pitcher Tony Mullane, who would ignore Walker's signals when he pitched to him. Baseball fans often jeered and yelled at Walker.

In 1887, Fleet Walker joined African American pitcher George Stovey on the Newark Little Giants, making them the first African American battery in organized baseball. Stovey won a record 35 games in one season with Walker behind the plate. In 1888, during the off-season, Walker played in Syracuse, but his baseball career would end when this team released him in July of the following year. It was around this time that the American Association and the National League began to adhere to Jim Crow practices in baseball. The first black baseball team was the Cuban Giants, formed in 1885, and the first black league was formed in 1920. In 1933, a new Negro national league was formed, and in 1937, the Negro American League was begun.

As the Negro teams and game venues expanded, promoters sought Owens's help. At first he thought they wanted him to play baseball for them, but he soon realized that they wanted him to help promote the game by racing against a horse. Having Owens run at the start of each game might draw a larger crowd for the game that followed. At first he refused, but then he decided to do it. He desperately needed the money. Yet it was a terribly painful decision for him. He had been a world-famous athlete, the only four-time Olympic gold medal winner in the history of the games, and now he was reduced to running against horses. But Owens did not want his family to know the extreme poverty he had experienced as a child, and no one else was offering him a job. As he saw it, he had no choice in the matter (Owens 1972). He would travel with teams like the Pittsburgh Crawfords and the Indianapolis Clowns, earning as much money as he could. He traveled across the United States and to Cuba for baseball games, and was paid five cents for every dollar that people spent to see him run. He later explained: "People say that it was degrading for an Olympic champion to run against a horse, but what was I supposed to do? I had four gold medals, but you can't eat four gold medals. There was no television, no big advertising, no endorsements then. Not for a black man, anyway" (as quoted in Schwartz 2005).

Since the horse, typically a thoroughbred, was often startled by the gunfire that signaled the beginning of the race, Owens usually had a good chance of winning. Yet this was not how he wanted to race. He hated every moment of the experience, feeling degraded and humiliated by the spectacle. At times, he was asked to race baseball players and other celebrities in the towns he visited, although he had to give them a lead in the race. While he never enjoyed this job, he hoped the earnings would eventually provide him with enough money to return to college. Owens felt that earning a degree would give him a new life and new options (Owens 1978).

In addition to running against horses, Owens pieced together other odd jobs and promotional deals to bring in money. He danced for a brief time in Harlem. He also announced the songs for a Consolidated Radio Artists 12-piece band that toured across the United States, for which he earned $75,000. Then he set up a group of traveling basketball players called the Olympians. Yet none of these seemed to satisfy him personally or professionally, and none seemed to meet his need to compete.

Just after the Olympics, Owens had his first taste of political campaigning. He voted Republican most of his life (Owens 1978). Many African Americans at the time were registered with the Republican Party. Some felt that it was still the party of Abraham Lincoln, who they credited with bringing an end to slavery, and many African Americans found that the Republican Party made it easier for them to register to vote. Owens believed the Republican Party had better economic policies, even though he admitted that the ways in which the Republicans restricted personal freedoms troubled him. Owens was well aware of the terrible inequities and utter despair that many African Americans faced on a daily basis. He lived it. But in public, he would not disclose his own personal suffering. Instead, he focused on the positive, taking a cautious position on racial issues and telling audiences that anything could happen in America if you worked hard enough. This position brought him support from white audiences who appreciated his cautious stance on race.

Owens endorsed Republican Alf Landon, a two-term governor in Kansas who was nominated to run for the U.S. presidency against incumbent Franklin Delano Roosevelt. Landon, who did not make many public appearances during his campaign, felt that Roosevelt was harming businesses through his New Deal policy, which instituted a series of social and economic reforms to bring relief and recovery to the country after the Great Depression. Landon also accused Roosevelt of being corrupt. Some claimed that Landon was prejudiced against African Americans, but Owens needed to earn money. He was promised between $10,000 and $15,000 for his campaign work (McRae 2002), and the publicity Owens received through the campaign might lead to other jobs. Landon lost the election by a landslide, losing the popular vote by more than 10 million. Later Owens reflected on the campaign, noting that it was the worst race he ever ran (McRae 2002).

In 1938, Owens and Ruth welcomed their second daughter, Beverly, to the family. While she was a source of joy to them, they faced significant problems throughout the year. Forkins was no longer his manager

(McRae 2002), and Owens's financial situation took a turn for the worse. On October 4, 1938, the federal government placed a lien of $746 against his house because he failed to pay income tax on the $10,000 he earned in the months after he returned from Germany (FBI 1956). Around this same time, he found work as a playground specialist in Cleveland. This job paid $28 a week, bringing in approximately $1,500 a year, which was barely enough to support a small family. Owens enjoyed the children who came to the playground, but they only reminded him that he wished to become a gym teacher and coach. He had realized so many of his dreams, most of which were so unlikely—going to college, winning gold at the Olympics—but this rather ordinary dream was out of his reach. So many people were able to become teachers, but how many had won four gold medals? He tried to keep himself in shape just in case he could compete again. He would run home each evening from the playground to maintain his fitness (Owens 1978).

Then, just over a year later, in May of 1939, Owens had more financial bad fortune. He declared voluntary bankruptcy. Owens was a cosigner on a note that was supposed to be used to produce a show in New York, but the other cosigner took the money and disappeared (McRae 2002). When he declared bankruptcy, he had $2,050 in assets, and $8,891 in liabilities (FBI 1956). Times seemed like they could not get worse, but Owens now had three young daughters to raise. Baby Marlene was born on April 19, and he needed to persevere.

BUSINESS VENTURES

Beginning in 1938, Jesse Owens operated a dry cleaning business on North High Street in Columbus. The Jesse Owens Dry Cleaning Company promised "Speedy Seven-Hour Service by the World's Fastest Runner." Owens (1978) explained that he decided to go into this venture when two men, who he only referred to as Nat and Jack, approached him about beginning the chain of dry-cleaning stores with them. Owens explained that at first the money poured in and he was able to pay off the mortgage on his parents' home. As the dry cleaning stores expanded from two to a dozen, he was able to buy a house for himself, Ruth, and his daughters. Then one day, there was a sign on one of the stores: Temporarily Closed. Owens was not able to find Nat or Jack. Something was terribly wrong.

As it turned out, Nat and Jack had used Owens's name to borrow money, and they paid Owens out of the borrowed sum to keep him from becoming suspicious. But the cleaning business never took hold, and the bills did not get paid. In the end, Owens, who was only 27 years old at the time, faced $114,000 in debt. He turned to his father for advice on what to do, and the two of them prayed, just as they prayed together when he was sick as a young boy. As the two men talked, Owens did some calculations. He figured that if he worked for 43 more years, he would need to earn $50 more each week to repay the money. Owens knew he could do it. He went to the bank with his father at his side to borrow the money he needed to cover the failed business. The bank granted him the loan, and in time he did pay off all the debt.

A BRIEF RETURN TO OHIO STATE

In 1940, Owens returned to Ohio State hoping to finish his degree so that he could become a physical-education teacher. He was still not ready to give up on this dream. He worked as an assistant trainer with the track team while he tried to finish the upper-level courses he needed to complete his degree. Unfortunately, Owens's studies did not go well. His grade point average was 1.07 out of 4.0, short of the 1.5 required for students to stay enrolled in the university. Owens did not know how to study, and the classes he needed to finish his degree were proving quite difficult. He was expelled in December 1940 and March 1941 for poor grades. On both occasions he was readmitted, but he was never able to achieve the grades he needed to stay enrolled at the university. Owens gave up on his dream to have a degree, and instead turned his attention to other ventures.

During this same time period, Owens returned to political campaigning. In November of 1940, in an unusual move given his commitments to the Republican Party, Owens endorsed Democratic President Franklin Delano Roosevelt, who was seeking his third term as president. It is not immediately clear why Owens supported Roosevelt. The president had widespread support from the labor unions, African Americans, Jews, Catholics, and leading intellectuals, and perhaps Owens agreed. By 1934, many African Americans in the North had begun aligning themselves with the Democratic Party (Kenneally 1993), and Roosevelt had begun to form a New Deal coalition that embraced African Americans. Still, it is unlikely that Owens was changing his political party. When he campaigned for Landon, Owens commented publicly, ". . . any of my race who votes the Democratic ticket is the lowest dog in the world" (Kenneally 1993, 123).

To demonstrate his support for Roosevelt, Owens offered to debate his good friend, boxer Joe Louis, who was campaigning for opponent Wendell Wilkie (FBI 1956). Wilkie campaigned against the New Deal and the government's lack of military preparedness. He blamed Roosevelt for employment inequities African Americans faced. After Roosevelt increased military contracts during the campaign, Wilkie accused him of warmongering (Eleanor Roosevelt Papers).

In spite of Owens's support for his third term, Roosevelt never publicly acknowledged Owens's accomplishments, supposedly because he feared a backlash from Southern voters (McRae 2002, 174). Roosevelt went on to win the election, defeating Wilkie by five million votes, but he would not seek out Owens until he needed him in the context of war.

THE WAR YEARS

On December 7, 1941, Japan launched attacks on Pearl Harbor, and the United States entered World War II. There were 2,335 American servicemen and 68 civilians who died in the attacks that day, as 18 U.S. naval ships and 170 American planes were destroyed. Roosevelt had campaigned for his third term with promises that he would do anything possible to prevent U.S. involvement in the war. In late 1940, when Japan occupied Indochina, Roosevelt provided more aid to the Republic of China and stopped supplying oil and other raw materials to Japan. However, he continued to negotiate with the Japanese in an attempt to avert U.S. entry into the war. Roosevelt pushed for the Lend-Lease Act of 1941, which allowed the United States to give supplies to any country that was vital to U.S. defense (i.e., the Allied nations). He had ordered U.S. warships to shoot on sight any Axis ships found between the United States and Iceland, including ships from major Axis powers such as Germany, Italy, and Japan. Yet when Japan attacked Pearl Harbor, public sentiment about the war swiftly changed and Roosevelt was left with no recourse. He declared war on Japan. On December 11, 1941, Germany and Italy declared war on the United States and the defeat of Nazi Germany became a top priority of U.S. war efforts, even though the U.S. had done little up to that point to deter Hitler's advances in Europe and his persecution of Jews and others throughout Europe. Once the U.S. declared war, over 18 million men and women served in the U.S. armed forces in World War II.

As the U.S. waged war in Europe and the Pacific, Americans struggled with economic problems and racial discrimination at home. War rations began in the spring of 1942, placing restrictions on foods such as butter, coffee, sugar, and beef. Families were restricted to one pound of coffee every five weeks (Lynch 2006). Women had to plan meals under these tight restrictions, and they often used home canning, their own "Victory" gardens, and other means to provide meals for their families. Rationing also affected gasoline and fuel oil, resulting in cutbacks on automobile usage and bus service. It was not acceptable for people to complain about these conditions; instead, those who wished to complain were reminded that the nation was at war, and everyone needed to contribute.

Some groups suffered more than others during the war. In February 1942, President Roosevelt signed Executive Order 9066 authorizing the U.S. Army to remove Japanese American citizens from the West Coast to internment camps (Zinn 2003). No warrant, indictment, or hearing was required. Nearly three-quarters of those imprisoned in the United States were American citizens who were born in the country. These actions remained largely out of the public eye until after the war ended.

The African American community also struggled against discrimination during the war. The community at large was not supportive of the war effort, even though there was no formal organized resistance to it. One African American university student at the time explained, "The Army jim-crows us. The Navy lets us serve only as messmen. The Red Cross refuses our blood. Employers and labor unions shut us out. Lynchings continue. We are disenfranchised, jim-crowed, spat upon. What more could Hitler do than that?" (Zinn 2003, 419). Those who served in the military did so in segregated units until 1948 when President Truman issued Executive Order 9981, which provided for equal treatment and opportunity in the armed forces. However, it was not until the end of the Korean War that full integration was achieved.

Many among the African American community felt indifferent about World War II because they recognized that it would do little to change the social conditions they faced. At the same time, however, more than one million African Americans served in the armed forces during the war, and countless others worked on the home front to support war efforts. When President Roosevelt created the Fair Employment Practices Committee (FEPC) in 1941, doors began to open for African Americans to find employment in industries that had government contracts. Executive Order 8802, which created this committee, prevented discrimination based on race, creed, color, or national origin. Although it was never signed into law, FEPC did help African Americans find employment in industries that had previously barred them from work during the war (The Eleanor Roosevelt Papers 2003).

Within this context, Jesse Owens was finally called to a meeting with President Roosevelt at the White House. He was asked to supervise the wartime hiring of Negroes at the Ford Motor plant in Detroit. Few African Americans had been able to work in plants such as this before the war, and Owens was asked to find the "right ones" (Owens 1978, 138). This meant he needed to find workers who would get along with the whites already working in the plant so that work could be done in a productive way and the war could be won. Owens was also asked to lead the Negro side of a new national fitness program led by the Department of Civilian Defense to boost the mental and physical health of African Americans in the wake of the war.

With these new opportunities on the horizon, Owens moved his family to Detroit, and seemed to enjoy his new work. The salary Owens earned in this new position was quite good, allowing him to pay off the loan for the failed dry-cleaning business by the war's end (Owens 1978). In addition to Owens's work with the Ford Motor Company, he traveled to Washington, D.C., regularly throughout this period, and he also was hired for various speaking engagements. During these war years, Owens faced pressure to condemn Hitler and claim that he went to Germany to beat him. Yet Owens was reluctant to do so. Instead, he would only admit that he went to Germany to run (McRae 2002, 232).

Jesse Owens suffered significant personal losses as the war raged abroad. First, his mother died. This was a terrible loss for Owens and his entire family. Emma had been a pillar of strength for all of them, but especially for him. He later wrote that his mother was the "kind of person who seemed like she'd never die" (1978, 122). He tried to comfort himself and his family, but it was difficult. He soon realized that his father was inconsolable. Seven months later his father, Henry, also died.

Then, after agonizing months with no correspondence, Owens received word that his good friend Luz Long had died in the war. Long and Owens had exchanged frequent and regular letters throughout the years after the Olympics, and Owens knew Long was enlisted to fight in the war. The last letter he received from his friend came as Long was engaged in battle in the North African campaign. Long wrote to Owens, telling him that his death was imminent. Long explained that he was not afraid to die, but he did fear for his wife and small son, and he seemed to regret that his son, Karl, would grow up without a father. In the letter, Long asked Owens to someday find Karl and tell him about his father, and to "tell him how things can be between men on earth" (Owens 1978, 119). Long died just a day or two after he wrote this final letter to Owens.

In the spring of 1945, the end of the war was brought about by Russian victories in Berlin, Allied successes in Europe, and the U.S. bombs on Hiroshima and Nagaski, which killed more than 150,000 Japanese civilians. Over 62 million people lost their lives during the war, with some of the worst atrocities committed against innocent civilians in German concentration camps and military prisoners of war held in Japanese camps.

THE WINDY CITY

After the war, Owens pushed himself to work harder, even though it was painful for him to be away from his family. The Ford Motor Company had begun to reorganize its staffing at the plant, and he decided that he could make more money working independently through his own businesses and speaking engagements. He had a small public-relations firm that offered consulting to various corporations and he gave motivational speeches across the country to various groups, including youth groups, which he particularly enjoyed. He was very personable, humble, and admired, making him popular with African American and white audiences alike. In part, Owens felt he needed to travel and do speaking engagements because he did not want to be poor again. Perhaps this fear is what drove him most. He did not want to "go back to being that Alabama sharecropper's starving son," and he did not want his daughters to experience the poverty he once knew (Owens 1978, 134). There were times when he would fly home, eat dinner with his family, and then fly out for another engagement that same evening. It was a fast-paced life, and he seemed unable to slow down. Although he was usually able to be home for special occasions like birthdays and holidays, he knew he missed out on the special things that happened on a day-to-day basis when he was gone.

In spite of his success as a public speaker, Owens missed his family immensely when he traveled. He often referred to Ruth and his daughters as his four gold medals, and he seemed to always treasure the time he had with them (Owens 1972). However, he hoped to find ways to work and earn money while staying closer to home. In 1949, Owens moved Ruth and his daughters to Chicago, where he thought they would have a better life. He initially took a job as sales director for Leo Rose Clothing, but he later quit the job out of frustration with the store's policy to give whites a 10 percent discount on every purchase (McRae 2002, 280). Shortly after this, he began to lead the Juvenile Delinquency Program for the Illinois Youth Commission. He later lost this job when he took a young man out of a juvenile home and helped him to find a job as a dishwasher. Owens had broken a policy as he tried to help this young man.

In 1950, national public attention turned yet again to Owens and his athletic accomplishments. On January 26, Owens was named the Greatest Athlete of the Past 50 Years in an Associated Press poll. This was a tremendous honor for Owens. He won by an overwhelming margin, earning nearly double the votes of the two athletes who came in second and third place behind him, Jim Thorpe and Paavo Nurmi, a Finn who was a notable middle- and long-distance runner (McRae 2002). Many people gathered in Chicago in the ballroom of the Sheraton Hotel to help him to celebrate this honor, including Avery Brundage and Daniel Ferris, the men who ended his track career in 1936. His friends and former teammates were there, including Dave Albritton, Ralph Metcalfe, Mel Walker, and Coach Larry Snyder, and of course Ruth and the girls were proudly at his side. Remarkably, the records he set at the 1936 Olympics still stood. The 200-meter and relay records would not be broken until the 1956 Olympics, and his record for the long jump would stand for 25 years.

RETURN TO BERLIN

In August of 1951, Jesse Owens appeared with the Harlem Globetrotters in the Berlin Olympic Stadium; it was the first time he returned to the city after the Olympic games. He originally joined up with the Globetrotters in 1949, giving short talks and running for the crowd that gathered to see the team compete. Now he accompanied the Globetrotters throughout Europe on a U.S. State Department tour. The group was going to Berlin in part because the State Department hoped to see changes in Berlin, including democracy and freedom for the city's residents. As he returned to the stadium, Owens wore his Olympic uniform and carried small American flags in each hand. He delivered a speech to the crowd of more than 75,000 people, who warmly greeted and cheered for the Olympic star.

As he was leaving the stadium, a young German boy asked him for an autograph. The picture he held for Owens to sign was that of Luz Long. As Owens looked at the boy, he realized the striking family resemblance. This was Karl Long, Luz's son. Finally, Owens was able to meet his friend's child, now a teenager, and tell the boy of the time he spent with his father, just as Long had asked in his last letter to Owens. It was a bittersweet time for them both as they became acquainted. The two visited the wall in the Olympic stadium where the 1936 Olympic athletes' names were inscribed. The old friends' names were still there.

GOVERNMENT SERVICE

From January until August of 1952, Owens worked as manager of the Wedgwood Towers Hotel at 6400 South Woodlawn Avenue in Chicago (McRae 2002). The hotel allowed both African American and white clientele, which was something that was not common in every Chicago hotel in the 1950s. Owens's teenage daughters would stop by to visit their father on occasion. The family lived less than two miles away at 6800 South Wabash Avenue.

In addition to these responsibilities, Owens found time to do community work at the South Side Boys Club, where he arranged to have Joe Louis and other notable people meet with the boys. Working with youth continued to be a main priority for Owens. While he was never able to realize his dream of becoming a schoolteacher and coach, Owens had certainly become a teacher to young people around the world through his outreach to youth clubs and groups.

While working at the hotel, Owens was approached by members of the campaign to elect William Stratton, a Republican known as Billy the Kid, as the next governor of Illinois. They had noticed his work with youth in Chicago, and they were interested in having him join their efforts. Stratton promised that, if Owens campaigned for him and he won, he would create an Illinois Youth Commission that Owens could lead. Owens agreed, Stratton won, and Owens had a new position with the Illinois Athletic Commission.

Owens assumed his new responsibilities in 1954, reporting to work at 160 North LaSalle Street in Chicago. He made $6,000 per year at this post (McRae 2002, 284). He was busier than ever before as he continued to host the jazz radio show, set up his own employment agency, and run his public relations firm. Owen continued to direct the boys' club, and he made regular personal appearances and gave speeches, often covering the travel costs himself. One speaking engagement during this time was particularly special. Owens gave the commencement address to the graduating class at East Technical High School, his alma mater (FBI 1956). He never seemed to slow down. The World's Fastest Man maintained a fast pace as he worked day and night to meet the responsibilities he assumed.

A year after he began to work for the state of Illinois, President Eisenhower named Jesse Owens as an ambassador of sports. Owens served as Eisenhower's personal representative to the 1956 Olympic Games in Melbourne, Australia. These were the first games to be held in the southern hemisphere, and the United States offered a strong showing, coming in second place behind the Soviet Union in the total medal count. Bill Russell led the U.S. basketball team to Olympic gold, consistently outscoring opponents by at least 30 points (Nelson 2005), and U.S. women's diver Pat McCormick won two medals, repeating her 1952 performance.

In addition to attending the Olympic games, President Eisenhower also asked Owens to represent the United States on a goodwill tour of India, Malaysia, and the Philippines. The U.S. government was interested in spreading positive messages about democracy, particularly since each of these countries seemed to be vulnerable to communism in some way. On this tour Owens led athletic clinics for children, and he gave inspirational speeches about democracy that conveyed his patriotic views about the United States. Owens later wrote that this particular job "took him back," forcing him to rely on what he did as an Olympic medalist rather than what he could do as a man in his 40s (Owens 1970).

In spite of Owens's ongoing public service to the state and federal government, as well as youth across the world, FBI director J. Edgar Hoover launched an investigation into Owens's private life. Investigators claimed this was necessary because Owens was being considered for a high-profile position in the government, but many people were suspicious. Hoover had a reputation for investigating people for political reasons, not necessarily because they were suspected of crimes, and nationally the Red Scare, along with Senator Joseph McCarthy and the House Un-American Activities Committee, had fostered a climate of suspicion and fear. Yet if Owens was concerned he did not mention it. In the end, he had nothing to fear. The investigation confirmed that Owens was not guilty of any crime or suspicious behavior (FBI 1956). The report noted only benign activities. In addition to a single traffic violation, there was mention that Owens sent greetings to the National Negro Congress during their second meeting in 1937, and that he was a guest of honor at a Youth Peace Crusade in Chicago in 1952, as was reported in the communist newspaper *Daily Worker*. A Detroit newspaper listed Owens among the membership of a Committee to Seek Unity of Racial Groups, and investigators noted that he was later a member of the Chicago Urban League. Otherwise, the investigation gave an account of Owens's employment history and the places he lived, and it listed his family members, including his wife and daughters' addresses and dates of birth. Owens's friends, business associates, neighbors, and other acquaintances were interviewed, and they spoke repeatedly of Owens's integrity, honesty, reliability, and good moral habits. Over the years, Owens consistently demonstrated that he was reputable and loyal to his country, and he spent his adult life sharing his patriotism and love for the United States. This loyalty became even more evident during the turbulent years of the 1960s.

Chapter 6

CIVIL UNREST AND THE BLACK FREEDOM MOVEMENT

Dear Mr. President. . . . There was only one question I couldn't answer during my ten-day stay in Ivory's capital city of Abidjan. It was asked by an educated teen-age boy over supper . . . "What about Eldridge Cleaver and Angela Davis?"

—Owens 1972, 99

Eldridge Cleaver and Angela Davis were controversial radicals and leaders in the black freedom movement. Cleaver, a convicted criminal and self-confessed rapist, helped to found the Black Panther Party and he served as the group's minister of information. In 1968, he ran as a candidate for president of the United States on the Peace and Freedom Party's ticket. That same year, he was involved in a skirmish between the Black Panthers and the Oakland city police, who brought a charge of attempted murder against him.

Angela Davis was an assistant professor of philosophy at the University of California–Los Angeles. The university's board of trustees, with Governor Ronald Reagan's support, dismissed Davis in a controversial ruling because of her affiliation with the Communist Party. Davis was also a member of the Black Panthers, and in August of 1970 she was charged as an accomplice to murder, kidnapping, and conspiracy after an incident in the Marin County Courthouse where Black Panther members failed to free James McClain and the Soledad Brothers. In the process, Judge Harold Haley was taken hostage and murdered, and two of the accomplices died in a police shoot-out. Davis went underground, but was found two months later and put in prison until her trial. Many celebrities, including

John Lennon, Yoko Ono, and the Rolling Stones, rallied behind Davis, and there was broad public support for her release. Two years later she was set free and exonerated on all charges.

When Owens was questioned about the situation by the young person from the Ivory Coast while on a visit for the U.S. government in the spring of 1971, Cleaver was living in exile in Algeria and France, and Davis's trial was still pending. Owens's book *Blackthink: My Life as Black Man and White Man* was published the year before, and people generally understood that Owens did not align himself with the revolutionary black power movements. Yet the question from the young man was provocative to Owens, and he realized that he had no easy answer. Owens understood that Cleaver and Davis symbolized the struggles of the African American community during the civil rights movement. He did not endorse the alleged violence of Cleaver and Davis, and he admitted that their positions frightened him (Owens 1972). Yet this did not mean he did not agree with their broader hopes to change the conditions African Americans faced in the United States. The 1960s and 1970s challenged Owens's views on race, racism, and conditions in the United States, and he faced pressure from the public to express his views on race. Some criticized his position, some misunderstood, and still others supported him.

These were complicated times and Owens was among those searching for solutions. In the midst of the turmoil and challenges, he continued to find comfort and great joy with his family and friends, along with time to reflect on his past and accomplishments.

REMINISCENCES

The 1960s began on a sentimental note for Jesse Owens. The popular television show "This is Your Life," hosted by Ralph Edwards, honored Owens on April 27, 1960. The format of the show involved identifying a guest, sometimes a celebrity and sometimes an ordinary person, and taking that person to the studio to provide a biography of his life. Throughout the show, the guest would be reunited with family members, old friends, and former acquaintances. Appearing on the episode honoring Owens were his old teammates Dave Albritton, Ralph Metcalfe, and Frank Wykoff. Perhaps the most poignant moment came when Owens was reunited with his old coach Charles Riley. Owens knew that it was this man who opened up opportunities for him perhaps more than any other.

Another continued source of pride to Owens was his daughters. One particularly special moment was when his youngest daughter Marlene was crowned Homecoming Queen at Ohio State in 1961. She was the first

African American woman to have this honor in the university's history. During the ceremony Owens told his daughter, "Remember Darling, this could only happen in America." He was so proud of her and what she had accomplished. After accepting the award, Marlene confessed to her father, "Paula should have won it, really. She's prettier than I am. If I hadn't been black or Jesse Owens's daughter, I think Paula would have been Homecoming Queen" (Owens 1972, 63). Owens appreciated his daughter's frank way of talking about life and race. He later wrote that Marlene was a beautiful person and that she could discuss difficult issues in ways that were beautiful and helped people to understand.

Marlene was the second Owens daughter to graduate from Ohio State, earning a bachelor's degree in social work in 1961, followed by a master's degree from the University of Chicago in 1978. Marlene's older sister Gloria earned a bachelor's degree in education in 1953 from Ohio State, and a master's degree in education from the University of Chicago. All three girls married within a few years of each other; Beverly was the first, who eloped to marry Donald Prather in 1957. Owens later wrote that Beverly was the most like him—a bit more rebellious than his other daughters, but with a good heart. Gloria was married shortly after to Malcolm Hemphill, an educator and administrator in the Chicago public schools. Owens recognized and deeply admired the contributions Gloria and Hemp made to the public school system and their hopes to bring change for young people through education. Marlene married Stuart Rankin, an advertising executive and businessman, and she worked with young people as a social worker.

Owens was clearly proud of his daughters, their accomplishments, and their contributions to making the world a better place. All three were involved in education and public service, and all helped Owens to see the world in new and different ways as they grew up, married, and raised their own families. Gloria and Hemp had two daughters together, as did Beverly and Donald. Marlene and Stuart had one son, Stuart Owen Rankin, who bore a striking similarity in appearance to his famous grandfather.

During the 1960s, Owens continued to work tirelessly with various business and athletic ventures. He formed the Owens-West & Associates public relations firm. He did commercials for a variety of products that kept his name and image in the public eye: Lucky Strike cigarettes, Quaker Oats, Tasty Tinned beef stew, Meister Brau beer, and others. In 1965, Owens served as a running coach for the New York Mets.

During this time, Owens, who had overcome his childhood illnesses and generally experienced good health as an adult, encountered a few health problems. Yet these did not seem to slow him down too much.

Owens had ulcers in his stomach, which caused him great pain at times, and then he developed a serious case of pneumonia. This illness caused him to be hospitalized, and some feared he wouldn't survive the illness. But he pulled through, just as he had so many years before as a young boy in Alabama. The main difference was that now he had Ruth, his daughters, and their husbands at his side.

Shortly after he recovered from pneumonia, Owens was golfing with Ralph Metcalfe and other friends when he injured his back. Several discs were out of place and Owens needed surgery. While he was reluctant to have surgery on his back, the pain was too intense and he knew that something would need to be done to take care of it. This was the first time he had ever faced surgery, and fortunately the operation was successful. Owens was back on the golf course just two months later, winning a tournament against some men who were half his age. Owens was proud of his accomplishment, and he put the golf trophy next to his gold medals (Owens 1978).

Owens typically spent very little time relaxing, but there were some things he enjoyed during his down time. In addition to golfing with his friends, he liked swing music and big band jazz (McRae 2002) and he regularly hosted radio shows that aired this music. While Owens was very involved with jazz, his favorite music was country and western. According to his daughter Marlene, he liked the stories in the songs. When he was home and had some time to relax, Owens would also watch sporting events or his favorite show, *Bonanza*, on television, and he enjoyed western movies.

In 1964, Owens also worked with Bud Greenspan to create the documentary *Jesse Owens Returns to Berlin*, which aired on 180 television stations across the United States. Although the film was made in 1964, it did not air until 1968 because ABC, CBS, and NBC thought it was too black for mainstream audiences (McRae 2002, 340). Owens narrated as he gave a tour of the stadium and reminisced on his Olympic experiences. His narration was interspersed with original film footage from Leni Riefenstahl's *Olympia*.

The 1960s were a time of accomplishment, success, and satisfaction for Owens. His daughters were raised and married and beginning families of their own, and he was able to spend time with his wife Ruth. He had provided a comfortable middle-class upbringing for his children, and had successfully protected them from the poverty he experienced as a young child. By all accounts Owens accomplished much in the decades that followed the Olympics. Owens's public relations work, his diplomatic work for the U.S. government, and his efforts to positively impact young people around the world brought him much personal and professional satisfaction. Finally it seemed like it might be time for Owens to relax and enjoy the benefits of his years of hard work. Unfortunately, this was not meant to be.

FURTHER FINANCIAL WOES

In spite of his business successes, Owens faced further financial difficulties in the 1960s. When he was 53 years old, Owens faced federal charges for failing to pay income tax on $59,024 he earned between 1959 and 1962. If found guilty, Owens would be required to pay a $40,000 fine and spend up to four years in prison. When word of the charges became public, Owens began to lose speaking engagements and other public-relations work. Business associates and some friends avoided him. Only his family stood by him.

In the weeks before the trial, Owens struggled with fear and shame. He had nightmares about his father's death. Finally, on the day before the trial, he flew to Oakville, Alabama (Owens 1978). But Oakville, which was no longer on the map, had changed considerably from the time young J. C. was nine years old. Sharecropping, which structured the land and social relations of Owens's youth, was no longer practiced, and new buildings dotted the land in places that once were fields and open spaces. Yet the visit was soothing for Owens. He was able to recall his youth and his father's prayer when he almost died as a young boy. He found peace again and was ready to face the consequences in court the next day.

When he went before Judge Sam Perry for income tax evasion, Owens pled nolo contendere (no contest). He would not lie or hide the truth. Owens knew he did not file the tax returns, and he did not plan to argue against the charges. Judge Perry fined him $3,000 ($750 for each year that he failed to file his tax return), and ordered him to repay the money he owed. The judge seemed to respect Owens's integrity and character, factoring this into his ruling in the case. He knew of the work Owens did throughout the world to promote democracy and goodwill. In the end, the judge did not sentence Owens to jail time or probation. Owens had a lot of money to repay, but he was grateful that he was free to work and earn the money he would need to compensate for his debt without going to jail.

CIVIL RIGHTS

April 4, 1968 was a day Jesse Owens would always remember. He was in New York City walking back to his hotel when he heard the terrible

news that Martin Luther King Jr. had been killed. Owens did not want
to believe it. King was one of the few people Owens considered to be his
hero (Owens 1972). Owens admired how King seemed to harbor no hate,
and that he seemed to not even know what hate was.

Owens had met Martin Luther King Jr. before he rose to the height of
his fame. During their first encounter, Owens spoke with King for a few
minutes after King gave a talk in New York. Of course King knew who
Owens was and was well aware of the famous athlete's accomplishments.
As they conversed, Owens conveyed his frustration with not being able
to return to school. King expressed his understanding, explaining that
Owens was like a child prodigy who could not continue with his work.
As the conversation continued, King advised Owens to build on what he
knew and loved (Owens 1970). Owens seemed to genuinely appreciate
these words of wisdom, and he interpreted this within the context of his
work with young people around the world. King's comments inspired him
to continue his youth outreach.

Owens clearly admired and respected Martin Luther King Jr., and he
referred to him as a saint. Yet Owens did not totally agree with King on
every social issue. In fact, Owens took issue with King over one of the
major concerns of the time, the Vietnam War. In *Blackthink*, Owens
wrote about his concern that King's comments on the war would be interpreted to mean that black men did not want to fight for their country.
Owens did not believe this was true, and he felt it was wrong to portray
this possibility.

Owens also disagreed with King most over the issue of nonviolence.
Owens felt there were times people needed to fight back, and he thought
that King should voice this as an option. Owens knew too well that there
were Hitlers in the world, and he did not believe that nonviolence would
work against people who were filled with hatred, fear, and violence.

Of course this position did not mean that Owens embraced violence.
His position was more complicated than saying violence was clearly right
or wrong. While Owens thought there were times when people needed to
fight back, he did not endorse those who were using what he believed was
largely unprovoked violence to bring social change. He wondered about the
young people in the 1960s who claimed to love everyone, yet stole or even
committed murder. In fact, Owens was more opposed to what he called
"blackthink," which he defined as "pro-Negro, antiwhite bigotry," (1970,
29) than he was to King's stance on nonviolence. Owens felt that blackthink was the same as whitethink, with similar consequences. He would not
agree with irrationality, violence, or bigotry by any person. Owens felt there
was no long-range vision for those who subscribed to blackthink.

Owens's views were certainly not naïve; he understood the challenges and significant problems many African Americans faced in the United States. From the time he was a child, Owens was well aware of violence against and mistreatment of African Americans in the United States. His grandparents had been slaves, as had their parents before them. He heard about the horrors of lynching, of African Americans being wrongly accused of crimes and unfairly punished. He remembered the atrocities of slavery, he knew the absurdity of Jim Crow laws, and he understood the ironies of war where black soldiers could die for their country but never enter the white United Service Organization (USO), nonprofit centers around the world that support military members and their families, without facing a court martial (Owens 1970). In spite of these problems, Owens never felt that hating white people was the solution. Instead, he felt that the problems African Americans faced were problems that many people faced. To Owens, poverty, prejudice, and violence were societal problems, not just African Americans ones.

At the same time, Owens recognized the changes that had occurred for African Americans in U.S. society, and he believed it was important to focus on these positive aspects, although they had been slow to arrive. Owens noted how his father's life was better than his great grandparents' life. Henry was able to pray openly and not fear a plantation owner who would expect to sleep with his wife, aspects of life that were taken for granted by Owens but were not guaranteed to his great grandparents. Owens had a longer life expectancy than his father or grandfather. In the 1950s, Owens had a jazz show for an all-white station on the radio. He had to be careful about what he played so that the show wouldn't be "tagged as Negro" (Owens 1970, 366), but he was still able to lead the show. Owens played a mixture of styles, including swing music by the African American Count Basie, and jazz music by the white pianist Dave Brubeck. By the 1970s, Owens had the same jazz program, but on a black station. Rather than just one station for African Americans, as in the early days of his radio work, there were more than 600 stations across the country with programming specifically for African Americans. The stations had 50 million dollars in advertising, African American performers doing advertising, and African American executives in charge (Owens 1970). Owens saw similar trends in television and other media.

Owens had seen significant social changes, but he knew that more were needed, even among African Americans. He witnessed lighter-skinned African Americans refuse to associate with darker-skinned African Americans. He knew that realizing a society where people were respectful of one another and nondiscriminatory in their actions and beliefs would be difficult to achieve. While he had no sweeping solutions to offer, he was sure that the approach of young militant African Americans would only bring trouble. Owens believed that African Americans had opportunities in the United States, and he felt that these opportunities, if realized, could make all the difference in society. By becoming members of universities, the workforce, and other social institutions formerly dominated by whites, Owens believed African Americans could disprove the myths and racist beliefs that so many whites held. To Owens, the only reason an African American would not succeed in the United States was because he or she chose to fail (Owens 1970).

It could be argued that Owens's position on race was more closely aligned with Booker T. Washington's views that blacks should seek economic independence rather than racial and social equality. Through economic independence, other changes could come. Owens was well aware that African Americans were not a single, monolithic cultural group. Instead, there were differences in their experiences, values, opinions, beliefs, and hopes. Owens felt that too much could be made of racial differences, and he wished for a world where less focus could be placed on the color of a person's skin, and more emphasis on their character, intellect, and abilities. Owens felt that most African Americans were not much different than he was; that is, they were simply trying to make ends meet and provide for their families as they attempted to make sense of a complicated world where wars raged, people went hungry, and jobs were hard to secure. Owens believed the militant blacks were among the minority, and that they risked returning America to its former segregated past. Yet he understood that some of these differences among African Americans were due to social class, and that Eldridge Cleaver's hate had something to do with growing up poor in the urban ghetto.

Owens's position on civil rights drew criticism from African Americans who felt that he should do more to help them gain more equitable treatment in American society. Some called Owens an Uncle Tom, a pejorative term for someone who was seen to be subservient to white authority. These criticisms were hard for Owens to bear, and they prompted him to write the book *Blackthink* with Paul Neimark.

Jesse Owens's daughters did not always agree with their father when they discussed civil rights issues in the 1960s and 1970s. The Owens girls joined in civil rights marches, and while their parents did not necessarily approve, they respected their daughters' positions (McRae 2002). Owens understood that this was a new generation, and he learned from his daughters as they read about and discussed civil rights issues. In fact, it was his daughter Gloria who gave him Eldridge Cleaver's book *Soul on Ice*. Owens later claimed that this book changed him. In spite of some differences of opinion, the Owens family all agreed with Martin Luther King Jr.'s hopes for justice and social change. In general, they felt that being involved and providing examples through their own lives would be the most effective way to bring these changes. It was up to individuals.

Owens's position on racism in the United States was challenged like never before in the context of the 1968 Olympic Games. Threats of boycotts brought reminders to him of the 1936 Olympics, and he was called upon to counsel and help advise the young athletes. There were no clear answers, and Owens spent a great deal of time questioning his own position, even after the Olympics ended. Owens did not support the idea of a boycott, and he felt the games should go on. This brought even more controversy his way as the Olympics neared.

OLYMPICS AND CONTROVERSY

Harry Edwards, a former discus thrower, was central in leading the 1968 Olympic boycott efforts. Edwards was a sociology instructor at San Jose State University where several of the Olympic athletes attended school, including track athletes Tommie Smith and John Carlos. In 1967, Edwards helped to organize African American student athletes at San Jose State in a series of rallies and protests designed to bring public attention to the racial injustices they faced. At the time, African American student athletes were being steered toward physical-education programs, not the humanities and sciences, and many found themselves living in hotels or dormitory lobbies because of racial discrimination. As a result of the protest activities, the student athletes were able to force changes that ensured that university housing would be open to all students, more African American faculty would be hired, and more African American students would be enrolled at the university (History San José 2005).

Edwards also helped to organize the Olympic Project for Human Rights (OPHR), which included student athletes who were potentially competing in the upcoming Olympics and high-profile celebrity athletes like Lew Alcindor (later known as Kareem Abdul-Jabbar), Muhammad Ali, Bill Russell, and Jim Brown. The group threatened to boycott the 1968 Olympic Games in Mexico City, Mexico. They insisted that six demands be fulfilled in order for the black athletes to participate in the games:

1. Restoration of Muhammad Ali's title and right to box in America
2. Removal of the anti-Semitic and antiblack Avery Brundage as president of the IOC
3. Banning of all-white teams and individuals from South Africa and Rhodesia
4. Addition of at least two black coaches to the U.S. men's Olympic track and field staff
5. Appointment of at least two black policymakers to the U.S. Olympic Committee
6. Complete desegregation of the bigot-dominated and racist New York Athletic Club

Jesse Owens took his most public and perhaps most controversial stand against militant black power protests in the prelude to and aftermath of the 1968 Mexico City Olympics. The IOC threatened to remove the entire U.S. Olympic team, reminding athletes that the games were not supposed to be used for political purposes. Owens publicly agreed that there was no room in athletics for politics, and he disagreed with the athletes about the need to boycott the Olympic games. Brundage wrote to Owens before the games, praising him for his stance against the proposed African American boycott.

Harry Edwards accused Jesse Owens of being a "bootlicking Uncle Tom." He put Owens's picture, along with photographs of Willie Mays and Rafer Johnson, on a bulletin board in his office with the title "Traitor (Negro) of the Week" (Hano 1968). Edwards's views about him clearly bothered Owens, and later in his book *Blackthink* Owens openly wondered if Edwards was correct, whether he had indeed helped to perpetuate the persistent inequalities in American society, particularly after Dr. Martin Luther King Jr.'s death. Owens struggled against his own anger in the wake of King's murder. Americans faced difficult issues in 1968 as the world struggled through turmoil, unrest, and conflict. As the war in Vietnam raged in spite of public protest, civil rights disturbances occurred on campuses across the country, Martin Luther King Jr. and Robert F. Kennedy were assassinated, student demonstrations and strikes in Paris and Mexico City resulted in bloodbaths and near anarchy. In spite of his personal struggles to make sense of the difficult issues the nation faced at this time, particularly with regard to civil rights, Owens stood firm, clearly stating his problems with Edwards and other militant black leaders. To

Edwards he wrote: "Harry Edwards, my name has never been Tom. But I *am* old enough to be your uncle. I know the trouble you've seen. Now can I make *you*—and everyone—see that it's nothing, absolutely nothing, next to the trouble you and your *blackthink* are about to make?" (Owens 1970, 23).

Many felt the accusations Edwards made against Owens were unfair and thoughtless. In a review of Owens's book *Blackthink*, A. S. Doc Young explained:

> Most black extremists who call older blacks or Negroes, Uncle Toms, have little knowledge, or understanding, of what older blacks have gone through, nor any substantial knowledge of the concrete contributions many of them have made, despite millstoning handicaps, to racial progress. Intolerant, they accept no philosophies other than their own. They forget that they operate from foundations laid down by the Jesse Owenses, who took horrifying amounts of guff from white bigots, but survived and, more than that, forget relentlessly ahead. (1970, 278)

Unlike Edwards, Owens was willing to hear the positions other people held and to consider them seriously. Sometimes this resulted in him changing his position, and other times it did not, but he never seemed to rule out another person's point of view without careful thought.

Owens attended the Olympic games, and he was asked to speak with the African American athletes to deter any potential for protest. In the end, the African American athletes did not boycott the Olympics in 1968, but the games did not end without incident. In spite of Owens's advice, Tommie Smith and John Carlos staged a protest when they won gold and bronze medals in the 200-meter race. When they took the medal stand, the two athletes raised their black-gloved fists in a black power salute as "The Star-Spangled Banner" played. Smith wore a black scarf around his neck as a symbol of black pride, while Carlos wore beads around his neck in remembrance of lynching victims. Both wore black socks and no shoes to symbolize poverty in the black community. Silver medalist Peter Norman from Australia joined in the protest by attaching an OPHR badge to his uniform when he took the podium. When the athletes left the medal podium, the crowd booed. Shortly after this, the Olympic Committee stripped them of their medals, barred the athletes from further competition, and sent them home. When they returned to the United States, rather than receiving a heroic welcome, the two were subjected to death threats and intense criticism.

Owens felt that their gesture at the Olympics was really unimportant in the end. He believed that in some ways the two had taken away from other members of the team who wished to stage a more organized protest. After the incident, Owens tried to keep Smith and Carlos from being expelled from the games, even though he did not agree with their actions. He personally understood how significant the consequences could be. But his efforts to salvage Smith and Carlos's status were not successful.

Owens believed that their protest accomplished nothing and gave a bad name to sports. He saw the protest as detracting from the accomplishments at the games. Many records were broken that year, in part because of the thin air of Mexico City's 7,349-foot altitude. Bob Beamon, a U.S. long jumper, leaped 29 feet, 2½ inches for the gold medal, beating the existing world mark by nearly two feet. Swimmer Debbie Meyer won three individual swimming gold medals. High jumper Dick Fosbury won gold with his signature backwards Fosbury flop. Al Oerter won his fourth consecutive discus title, and Wyomia Tyus became the first woman to win back-to-back gold medals in the 100 meters. Tyus dedicated her team's victory in the 4 × 100-meter relay to Smith and Carlos.

Some people criticized Owens for having views that appeared to be sympathetic to white people, but it seems that his points were often misunderstood. Young captured Owens's point and the controversy on his position well. Young wrote:

> Harry Edwards is a beneficiary of a Jesse Owens who, during his 57 years, has had a thousand good reasons for giving up, yet never did. It surely wasn't easy for this sickly son of an illiterate Alabama sharecropper to make it to the top. He made it because there was something great in him and because he had help from blacks (his impoverished family to begin with) and whites. And, now, he has the guts to be grateful. He writes, at times, like a public relations man for the Caucasian race. But his intentions are good. He intends to show that there are many good whites in America and that both races need each other. (1970, 278)

Although some people felt that Jesse Owens only went along with the status quo, simply accepting things the way they were, this was not necessarily true. There was plenty he did not agree with, and he was not afraid to let people know. Owens was not impressed with Hoover's emphasis on law and order, rather than justice and freedom, and he did not agree with Nixon's practices, including wiretapping (Owens 1970). Owens did not agree with the Vietnam War, and he stated so publicly. He felt that World War II was justified. The Japanese attacked the United States, and Hitler committed unspeakable atrocities, and to Owens this provided enough reason for the United States to enter the war. Yet, he could not find a good reason for the United States to be engaged in Vietnam.

UNDERSTANDINGS

Jesse Owens understood that people did not always appreciate him. When people close to him misunderstood him, he wanted to "walk and talk," to have dialogue so that better understandings could be developed. This was the approach that his coach Charles Riley had used, and Owens came to appreciate the value of just walking and talking. He also came to appreciate that ideas could be changed, and he was not afraid to have his ideas challenged. Instead, he seemed to take pride in the changes that occurred in his life and in the new understandings he developed. He appreciated efforts to make society more just and equitable, and while he did not always agree with the younger generation about how that could be accomplished, he was able to understand their point of view.

Owens's change in position from *Blackthink* to his later book *I Have Changed* was not as radical as that of Eldridge Cleaver. When Cleaver returned to the United States in 1975, he renounced the Communist Party and became a member of the Republican Party and an evangelical Christian. He did not stay as consistent with his original position as Angela Davis, who continued her life as a radical and activist, writing books and giving lectures around the world. Owens continued to learn and reflect on his views, articulating his concerns and possibilities for change. In particular he found hope in the community practices he observed in Abidjan, the capital city of the Ivory Coast (1972, 115). One of Owens's favorite books was Thoreau's *Walden*. He reread it several times, and seemed to be drawn to the quote: "It is not so important that many should be good, as that there be some absolute goodness somewhere, for that will leaven the whole lump" (as quoted in Owens 1970, 21).

Chapter 7

FINAL GLORY

Life is no sprint. It's a marathon—a long, long, long-distance race over hills and through valleys, sometimes even with stops along the way, and it's how you run that marathon, not how soon you get to the finish line, that matters.

—Owens 1972, 83–84

The Alabama Sports Hall of Fame, located in Birmingham, inducted its inaugural class of athletes in 1969. The primary purpose of the museum was to celebrate and preserve the sports heritage of the state. The first athletes to be honored included football greats Johnny Brown, Paul Bryant, Michael Donahue, James Hitchcock, Donald Hutson, James "Shug" Jordan, and Frank Thomas. Only one athlete inducted in the inaugural class was not a football star—boxer Joe Louis Barrow, the Brown Bomber. The second group of inductees in 1970 included a slightly broader variety of athletes: baseball stars Joseph "No Strike Joe" Sewell and Early "Gus" Wynn; football greats Henry "Hustlin' Hank" Crisp, John Heisman, William "Bully" van de Graaff, and Wallace Wade; and track stars Wilbur "Coach" Hutsell and Jesse Owens.

This was clearly one of the most significant honors Jesse Owens received during this period of his life. The recognition by his home state was a nostalgic honor, given to those athletes who brought fame and glory to the state of Alabama through their accomplishments. Joe Louis traveled to Alabama with Jesse Owens when his good friend was inducted into the hall of fame. Sharing the special occasion was bittersweet for the two men. By this time, Louis was suffering greatly from a mental breakdown. Gone was the Joe Louis that Owens had known and loved for so long. It was difficult for Owens to see his old friend this way. A few weeks after the ceremony Louis was in a mental hospital, a broken man after years of taking punches, fighting a cocaine addiction, and struggling against paranoia. Owens would stand by his friend through these difficult times, visiting him in the hospital and comforting Louis's wife Martha as best as he could. The two men always shared some good laughs when they got together, a pattern that continued even during this difficult time. One favorite source of humor was the story of the time when a guest at the hospital pointed out Louis to a visitor by mistakenly explaining how Louis had knocked out Max Schmeling in Berlin and Hitler had stormed out of the stadium (McRae 2002).

The last decade of Jesse Owens's life brought bittersweet contentment as he reflected on his own life and graciously received accolades that were in some cases long overdue. Owens loved to be with his family most of all, particularly his children and grandchildren, but as he grew older and his brothers and sisters passed away, he experienced an acute sense of loss. Owens continued to stay in close contact with his old friends, many whom were quite accomplished and well respected. Dave Albritton had become head of a bank in Ohio. Ralph Metcalfe, who served in the armed forces during World War II and coached track for Xavier University in New Orleans, became involved in Chicago politics and attempted to change conditions for African Americans in the city. Metcalfe worked first as an alderman on Chicago's South Side, and then in the U.S. House of Representatives as a cofounder of the Congressional Black Caucus. Of course Owens's closest and dearest friend was Joe Louis. The two men had a terrific history together, having coming into American sport when the American public's imagination was ready to be captured by African American athletes (Owens 1970). Owens and Louis shared experiences only the two of them could fully appreciate, carrying the responsibility of representing the African American athlete to the United States and the world, and sharing the private pain that accusations of "Uncle Tom" brought to each. They were the most visible African American athletes in their day, and while they both were known to wear smiles in public, they both knew suffering caused by the racism they faced. Owens later wrote that it was Louis who changed him most in his life (Owens 1972). It is easy to imagine that Owens changed Louis as well, just as he changed life for many others through his own accomplishments and goodwill.

SPORTS AND SOCIETY

Jesse Owens witnessed great changes in American professional sports across his life and career. As he grew older, he saw more African American athletes playing sports than he could ever have imagined when he competed in the 1936 Olympics. A particularly memorable moment was in 1947 when Jackie Robinson became the first African American man to play major league baseball. Robinson credited Joe Louis and Jesse Owens with paving the way for him (McRae 2002). Throughout the twentieth century, participation in university sports became more available for African Americans, which opened the path for scholarships as well as increased potential for amateur and professional competition in sports. Finally, it seemed that times could be changing for African American athletes.

Jesse Owens's contribution to the trend of increased African American participation in sports did not go unnoticed. Athletes like Robinson publicly praised Owens for his contributions and for serving as a role model. Track star Carl Lewis referred to Owens as his hero. Lewis's father had been well aware of Owens's accomplishments and had become acquainted with him. As a result, he encouraged his son to compete in track events just as Owens had. Young Carl began his track career by focusing on the long jump, and then he expanded to run the 100- and 200-meter races. Lewis was the first American to duplicate Owens' four-medal sweep, winning gold in the same events in the 1984 Olympics.

Owens was still getting attention in the media. In 1971, Arthur Daley wrote a piece for the New York Times entitled "Was Jesse Owens Really a Slowpoke?" The article focuses on the sense of humility that Owens carried throughout his life. In the article, Daley recounted a conversation with Owens where the former track star noted that his winning time in the 100 would have put him in eighth place in the 1968 Olympics. Daley proceeded to explain that Owens was incorrect, that his 10.3-second winning time would not even have allowed him into the finals. In fact, Owens would not have made the relay team, and he would have only placed sixth in the long jump. However, Daley noted that records are made to be broken, and he reminisced about the beauty of seeing Owens run. He concluded that Owens's long-jump record standing for 25 years was really a record in itself.

Owens certainly was a long-standing role model and hero to many American athletes. A decade after Owens's death, in 1990, President George H. W. Bush acknowledged Jesse Owens's influence when he awarded the Congressional Gold Medal posthumously to Owens. In his remarks, President Bush used Harrison Dillard, a track athlete from Cleveland, as one example of Owens's efforts and influence. In 1941, Jesse Owens gave Dillard a new pair of track shoes as he competed in the Ohio State high school track championship. That same day, Dillard won two state titles. Then in 1948, Dillard went on to win gold in the Olympics in the 100-meter dash, following in the steps of his idol.

Jesse Owens felt that sports gave African American children hope that they could realize the American Dream (Owens 1970). He encouraged young athletes like Carl Lewis to have fun and enjoy sports, and he saw sports as a way to gain entry into universities and other sectors of American life. Indeed, it was sports that had offered new possibilities for him when he was a young man, and he felt this would be a way for African Americans to progress even further in American society. Jesse Owens readily dismissed arguments made by authors like Jack Olsen, who wrote *The Black Athlete: A Shameful Story* (1968) and a series of articles for *Sports Illustrated Magazine* about racism in American sports. Olsen focused on the discrimination black athletes faced as they played on college and professional teams, and he felt strongly that racism would destroy America. Olsen did not agree with the commonly held view that African American athletes were content with their positions serving white coaches and fans who saw them as politically harmless entertainers. While Owens felt Olsen had the facts straight about African American athletes, he did not believe Olsen understood histori-cally how far African Americans had come. Rather than focusing on the fact that there were no black managers and only one black quarterback in professional football, Owens felt the focus should instead be placed on the many African American athletes who were actually involved in playing ball, and the increase in numbers from just a few decades earlier.

As he grew older, Owens became thoughtful and reflective, seeking to make sense of his experiences. During this time that he turned to writing and worked with Paul Neimark to pen his autobiography. Once this was completed, he set out to convey his thoughts on race, racism, and American society, beginning first with *Blackthink* in 1970, which he followed closely with *I Have Changed* in 1972. Writing can be a way to make sense of diffi-cult issues, yet sometimes more questions arise as deeper understandings are developed. Owens conceded: "I've still got more questions than answers. One reason I had some of the wrong answers was that for many years, un-fortunately, some of the *wrong* answers worked for me" (Owens 1972, 84). Owens did not elaborate on what his wrong answers were; instead, he pro-ceeded to tell the story of a young boy who read his autobiography. The boy wondered if it was ever boring for Owens to win all the time. Owens laughed when the boy asked the question, but later he became philosophical about it. He remembered that he never lost when it really meant something.

As Owens worked to better understand difficult issues of race and racism in the United States, he continued to learn and to reconsider what he previously believed. He no longer dismissed the claims made by leaders of the civil rights movement, and he knew that while soci-ety had come a long way since the days of slavery and sharecropping, there was still a long way to go. He struggled with making sense of how changes could come about. These struggles and the subsequent contributions he made through his writing resulted in Owens contributing to the national dialogue on civil rights. While not everyone agreed with him, his ideas sparked controversy, discussion, and thought. Later, Owens was named among the most influential African Americans in the United States, including mention in *The Black 100*, a formidable list of key African Americans in the struggle for equality compiled by writer Columbus Salley. While the list is not without problems, particularly because of the omission of some key contemporary leaders, Owens's name is 56th in the list, putting him clearly among those who contributed to the struggle for civil rights. Others on the list include Martin Luther King Jr., who was ranked first, followed by Frederick Douglass, Booker T. Washington, and W.E.B. DuBois. Other historical figures included Eldridge Cleaver, Langston Hughes, Joe Louis, Sojourner Truth, and Malcolm X, along with contemporaries like Oprah Winfrey, Colin Powell, and Toni Morrison.

ACCOLADES AND PRESIDENTIAL HONORS

Jesse Owens received another special honor just two years after being inducted into the Alabama Sports Hall of Fame. In 1972, The Ohio State University awarded Owens with an honorary doctorate in athletic arts. An honorary degree is recognition of a person's accomplishments and contributions to society. For the ceremony, Owens was able to finally don the university graduate's cap and gown, and he was hooded with the Ohio State colors as students, alumni, and dignitaries looked on. At last, he had a college degree.

Even though FDR did not invite Jesse Owens to the White House after his Olympic victories in 1936, other U.S. presidents would come to recognize his accomplishments and contributions. President Gerald Ford awarded Owens the Medal of Freedom in 1976, the highest award given to private citizens. In 1979, Owens was awarded the Living Legend Award by President Jimmy Carter. Carter summarized Owens's contributions: "A young man who possibly didn't even realize the superb nature of his own capabilities went to the Olympics and performed in a way that I don't believe has ever been equaled since . . . and since this superb achievement, he has continued in his own dedicated but modest way to inspire others to reach for greatness" (The Jesse Owens Foundation).

Finally, in 1990, Ruth Owens accepted the Congressional Medal of Honor from President Bush on her late husband's behalf.

CROSSING THE FINISH LINE

Throughout his life, Owens always tried to stay in good physical shape. In fact, he was able to wear his Olympic shorts and tank through most of his adult life. In his later years, Owens walked two miles every morning, and he swam and lifted weights to keep in shape. He did not run though. He explained, "I don't jog because I can't run flat-footed. And at 60 years old you're crazy to be out there running" (Litsky 1980).

Yet his good health would not last forever. In 1979, Owens was diagnosed with lung cancer. He had started to smoke when he was 32 years of age, often smoking a pack of cigarettes each day. Owens was first hospitalized at Good Samaritan Hospital in Phoenix, but most of his treatment during his illness was from the Tucson hospital. Owens served on the board of Phoenix Memorial Hospital, and the medical facility was later named for Jesse Owens, along with the street adjacent to the medical center.

Jesse Owens died at University Hospital in Tucson on March 31, 1980 at age 66. His wife Ruth was at his side. A memorial service was held for Owens in the Arizona State Capitol rotunda in Phoenix where thousands came to pay their respects. Then he was flown to Chicago, where he was buried in the Oak Woods Cemetery on Chicago's South Side. The grave has a patch of flowers and a tiny American flag. The main tombstone reads:

Jesse Owens
Olympic Champion
1936
    Athlete and Humanitarian, a master of the spirit as well as the mechanics of sports. A winner who knew that winning was not everything. He showed extraordinary love for his family and friends. His achievements have shown us all the promise of America. His faith in America inspired countless others to do their best for themselves and their country.
    September 12, 1913   March 31, 1980

The Reverend Jesse Jackson attended the funeral. Jackson had a unique connection to Owens and his good friend Joe Louis. When he was born in 1941 his parents had named him Jesse Louis Jackson in honor of the two heroes (McRae 2002, 372), a tribute to the significance the two men held in the United States at the time.

Owens's obituary in the *New York Times* reported that he traveled more than 200,000 miles each year and earned more than $100,000 annually.

President Carter eulogized Owens, "Perhaps no athlete better symbolized the human struggle against tyranny, poverty and racial bigotry" (Jesse Owens Foundation).

The racism that Owens tried to change through his example and participation still continued after his death. On the day after Owens died, William Shockley recommended that birth rates among poor Southern blacks should be restricted. The 1980s and 1990s brought little change to poor African Americans in urban and rural America as inadequate schools and housing, limited employment opportunities, and segregation and discrimination continued. This was perhaps most evident in the aftermath of Hurricane Katrina as the lack of resources and efforts to aid the poor was blatantly obvious in the suffering of the residents of New Orleans. In sports, African American athletes still faced discrimination, particularly as they attempted to break into traditionally white sports and white roles in sports. Hank Aaron, Michael Jordan, and others achieved fame and accomplishments in the midst of these conditions, but not without public scrutiny and personal suffering. Yet it is hard to imagine that Jesse Owens would be discouraged by any of this. Instead he would focus on the gains that have been made, and he would continue to strive to create better conditions for all people throughout the United States.

HOW HE RAN THE RACE

After Owens's death, various honors and remembrances kept Jesse Owens in the public's eye and thoughts. All speak to the impact he had throughout the United States and the world (see Appendix 3).

One of the more notable awards was instituted in 1981 when the USA Track & Field Association began to present an award annually to outstanding U.S. male and female athletes in Owens's honor. The Jesse Owens Award is considered to be the highest accolade in the sport. Past winners have including Marion Jones, Gail Devers, Michael Johnson, Jackie Joyner-Kersee, Edwin Moses, and Carl Lewis (for a complete list see Appendix 2).

The Ohio State University campus has many honors to the former student and athlete. There is a plaza with Jesse Owens's name and a sculpture with the inscription:

James Cleveland (Jesse) Owens 1913–1980
Jesse Owens's incomparable achievements as an Ohio State and Olympic athlete are legendary. He carried the name of this university and this country to world acclaim.

Three recreation facilities were built in 1976 as tributes to the famous athlete: the Jesse Owens Recreation Center South, the Jesse Owens Recreation Center North, and the Jesse Owens West Tennis Center. In 1998, construction began on the Jesse Owens Memorial Stadium, one of the most notable facilities of its kind in the country. The stadium, located on Fred Taylor Drive, was completed in 2001. It currently seats 10,000 people, hosting track and field, lacrosse, and soccer events throughout the year. Most notably, the athletic department hosts the Jesse Owens Classic each spring, which attracts the nation's top track and field athletes.

In 1980, Ruth Owens, along with her daughters, sons-in-law, and friends, formed the Jesse Owens Foundation. The foundation provides information and materials about Jesse Owens's life, and it strives to perpetuate the ideals and life work of Owens. Since 1983, more than 350 youth have benefited from this program. The Ruth and Jesse Owens Scholars Program provides scholarships to young people to attend Ohio State. In 2003, the foundation's scholarship program was endowed to Ohio State and renamed the Ruth and Jesse Owens Scholars Program at The Ohio State University. Owens's three daughters serve on the board for the foundation.

Jesse Owens's influence is still evident today. In 2007, *Runner's World* magazine ran a feature story on Owens that included photographs of the young Olympic champion and excerpts from writer Jeremy Schapp's newly released biography *Triumph: The Untold Story of Jesse Owens and Hitler's Olympics* and photographs from the 1936 Olympics in Berlin. Schapp claimed that he wished to write the biography on Owens because he was the most accomplished Olympic athlete of all time, and perhaps one of the most famous athletes ever. Yet Schapp realized that while people all around the world had a general sense of who Owens was, many believed myths about the athlete. Schapp wanted to set the story straight, particularly the story about Owens's accomplishments in the 1936 Berlin Olympics (*Runner's World* 2007).

By all accounts, Jesse Owens lived a remarkable life. His athletic accomplishments, which took only a matter of minutes in the 1936 Berlin Olympics, changed not only the course of his own life, but also the lives of others. He spread hope that African Americans could have full and equal participation in American society. As his writing reflects, Owens lived a humble life; he understood the enormity of his accomplishments, but also honestly recognized his personal shortcomings and mistakes. As he grew older, he continued to learn and to grow and to consider new possibilities for himself and others. We can only aspire to do the same. As Owens once said, "It all goes so fast, and character makes the difference when it's close" (Jentry 1989).

Appendix 1

AFRICAN AMERICANS WHO COMPETED IN THE 1936 OLYMPIC GAMES

Men

Dave Albritton
John Brooks
James Clark
Cornelius Johnson
James LuValle
Ralph Metcalfe
Jesse Owens
Frederick Pollard
Matthew Robinson
John Terry
Eddie Tolan
Archie Williams
Arthur Wilson
Jackie Wilson
John Woodruff

Women

Tidye Pickett
Louise Stokes

Appendix 2

WINNERS OF THE JESSE OWENS AWARD (USA TRACK & FIELD ASSOCIATION)

The Jesse Owens award has been presented each year since 1981 to the outstanding male and female track and field performers (see http://www.usatf.org).

Year	Male Winner	Female Winner
2005	Justin Gatlin	Allyson Felix
2004	Justin Gatlin	Joanna Hayes
2003	Tom Pappas	Deena Drossin Kastor
2002	Tim Montgomery	Marion Jones
2001	John Godina	Stacy Dragila
2000	Angelo Taylor	Stacy Dragila
1999	Maurice Greene	Inger Miller
1998	John Godina	Marion Jones
1997	Allen Johnson	Marion Jones
1996	Michael Johnson	Gail Devers

Year	Winner
1995	Michael Johnson
1994	Michael Johnson
1993	Gail Devers
1992	Kevin Young
1991	Carl Lewis
1990	Lynn Jennings
1989	Roger Kingdom

1988   Florence Griffith Joyner
1987   Jackie Joyner-Kersee
1986   Jackie Joyner-Kersee
1985   Willie Banks
1984   Joan Benoit
1983   Mary Decker
1982   Carl Lewis
1981   Edwin Moses

Appendix 3

TRIBUTES TO JESSE OWENS

Schools Named in Honor of Jesse Owens

Elementary Schools

Gueydan, Louisiana
Chicago, Illinois
New York, New York

High Schools

Cleveland, Ohio
Berlin-Lichtenberg, Germany

Cities with Streets Named in Honor of Jesse Owens

Berlin, Germany
Phoenix, Arizona
Abidjan, Ivory Coast

U.S. Postage Stamps Issued in Honor of Jesse Owens

1990
1998

Athletic Awards in Honor of Jesse Owens

- Jesse Owens Award (USA Track & Field Association)
- Jesse Owens International Trophy, presented by Herbert Douglas Jr. after Owens's death to honor an amateur athlete. Lance Armstrong was given the award in 2000.

Other Awards and Honors

- Jesse Owens Playground, New York City
- Owens Park, Chicago, Illinois
- Jesse Owens Sportsmanship Award (The Jesse Owens Foundation)
- In 1994, a plaque was placed in front of Owens's old home in Columbus at 292 South Oakley Street by his old neighbor and friend Earl "Wimpy" Potts.
- Jesse Owens Museum and Park in Lawrence County, Alabama
- The Ohio State University named a track and three recreational buildings in honor of Jesse Owens.

BIBLIOGRAPHY

Alabama Department of Archives and History. "Teacher Resources: Slave Code of 1833." Alabama Department of Archives and History. Available at: http://www.archives.state.al.us/teacher/slavery/slave1.html. Accessed August 2, 2006.

Center for Business and Economic Research, The University of Alabama. 1999. "Alabama's Changing Economy through the Twentieth Century." *Alabama Business and Economic Indicators* 68 (12). Available at: http://cber.cba.ua.edu/pdf/ab1299.pdf. Accessed August 9, 2006.

Clowser, Jack. 1952. "For World Sports." Jesse Owens Museum. Available at: http://www.jesseowensmuseum.org/index.cfm?fuseaction=res_viewDetails&id=26. Accessed October 9, 2006.

Daley, Arthur J. 1936. "Athletes Give Pledge to Keep Fit as Officials Warn against Making Trip a Joy Ride—Training Starts, but Seasickness Keeps Many in Berths—Smallwood's Condition the Same." *New York Times* (16 July): 12.

Digital History. 2006. "The Great Migration." Available at http://www.digitalhistory.uh.edu/database/article_display.cfm?HHID=443. Accessed August 19, 2006.

The Eleanor Roosevelt Papers. 2003. "Fair Employment Practices Committee." *Teaching Eleanor Roosevelt*, ed. Allida Black, June Hopkins, et. al. Hyde Park, New York: Eleanor Roosevelt National Historic Site. Available at: http://www.nps.gov/archive/elro/glossary/fepc.htm. Accessed April 7, 2007.

The Eleanor Roosevelt Papers: The Human Rights Years. "Wendell Wilkie: 1892–1944." Available at: http://www.gwu.edu/~erpapers/abouteleanor/q-and-a/glossary/wilkie-wendell.htm. Accessed January 1, 2007.

FBI. 1956. "Federal Bureau of Investigation Freedom of Information/Privacy Acts: Jesse Owens." Available at: http://foia.fbi.gov/owens_jesse/owens_jesse_part01.pdf. Accessed December 28, 2006.

Fleming, Thomas C. 1999. "A Party for Jesse Owens." Free Press (23 Jun). Available at: http://www.freepress.org/fleming/flemng78.html. Accessed November 18, 2006.

Greenburg, Jan Crawford. 1996. "Salute to Jesse Owens: Healing an Old Wound." Chicago Tribune (24 July). Available at: http://131.204.108.36/JOM/articles/art40.html. Accessed May 21, 2006.

Hano, Arnold. 1968. "The Black Rebel Who 'Whitelists' the Olympics." New York Times (12 May): SM32.

History San José. 2005. "Black Power (1964–1969)." The Speed City Era: An Exhibit from History San José. Available at: http://www.speedcityera.com/blackpower.html. Accessed January 2, 2007).

Jentry, T. 1989. Jesse Owens: Champion Athlete. New York: Bancroft Sage Publications.

The Jesse Owens Foundation. "Who is Jesse Owens." The Jesse Owens Foundation. Available at: http://www.jesse-owens.org/about5.html. Accessed January 1, 2007.

Johnson, R. 1995. "Torch Sheds Light on Jesse Owens Birthplace." Atlanta Journal (6 August). Available at: http://131.204.108.36/JOM/articles/art46.html. Accessed May 21, 2006.

Kenneally, James J. 1993. "Black Republicans During the New Deal: The Role of Joseph W. Martin, Jr." The Review of Politics 55 (1): 117–39.

Litsky, Frank. 1980. "Jesse Owens Dies of Cancer at 66; Hero of the 1936 Berlin Olympics." New York Times (1 April). Available at: http://www.nytimes.com/learning/general/onthisday/bday/0912.html. Accessed January 1, 2007.

Lynch, George Gilbert. 2006. "Christmas in Bakersfield During World War II." Bakersfield Californian (15 December). Available at: http://www.bakersfield.com/241/story/89616.html. Accessed December 31, 2006.

Mandell, Richard. 1971. The Nazi Olympics. Champaign, Ill.: University of Illinois Press.

McDaniel, Deangelo. 2005a. "New York Reporter Researching Owens Book." Decatur Daily News (27 June). Available at: http://www.decaturdaily.com/decaturdaily/news/050627/book.shtml. Accessed August 12, 2006.

McDaniel, Deangelo. 2005b. "The Forgotten Side of Jesse Owens: Olympic Great's Cousins Say Link to Fitzgeralds, Alexanders Untold." *Decatur Daily News* (27 June). Available at: http://www.decaturdaily.com/decaturdaily/news/050627/owens.shtml. Accessed August 12, 2006.

McRae, Donald. 2002. *Heroes without a Country: America's Betrayal of Joe Louis and Jesse Owens*. New York: HarperCollins.

Nelson, Murry R. 2005. *Bill Russell: A Biography*. Greenwood Biographies. Westport, Conn.: Greenwood Press.

New York Times. 1932. "Miss Walsh Equals Olympic Sprint Mark; Ties 100-meter Record and Also World's 50-Meter Time in Cleveland Trials." (12 June): S3.

New York Times. 1933. "World Mark in 100 Tied by School Boy." (17 June): S4.

New York Times. 1936. "United States Olympic Team Sails for Games Amid Rousing Send Off." (16 July): 1.

Ohio High School Athletic Association. "History of OSHAA." Available at http://www.ohsaa.org. Accessed October 9, 2006.

Olsen, Jack. 1968. *The Black Athlete: A Shameful Story*. New York: Time-Life Books.

Owens, Jesse. 1976. *Track and Field*, ed. Dick O'Connor. Hartford: Connecticut Printers.

Owens, Jesse, and Paul G. Neimark. 1970. *Blackthink: My Life as Black Man and White Man*. New York: Morrow.

Owens, Jesse, and Paul G. Neimark. 1972. *I Have Changed*. New York: Morrow.

Owens, Jesse, and Paul G. Neimark. 1978. *Jesse: The Man Who Outran Hitler*. Reprint, New York: Ballantine Books, 1983.

Pacey, Leslie Farrey. 1996. "Owens Park Marvelous Says Daughter of Legend." Jesse Owens Museum. Available at: http://www.jesseowensmuseum.org/index.cfm?fuseaction=res_viewDetails&id=58. Accessed May 21, 2006.

PBS. 2003. "Reconstruction: The Second Civil War." PBS. Available at: http://www.pbs.org/wgbh/amex/reconstruction/sharecrop/index.html. Accessed August 9, 2006.

Raatma, Lucia. 2004. *Jesse Owens: Track and Field Olympian*. Chanhassen, Minn.: The Child's World.

Riefenstahl, Leni. 1992. *Leni Riefenstahl: A Memoir*. New York: Picador.

Riley, James A. 1983. *The All-Time All-Stars of Black Baseball*. New York: TK Publishers.

Rooney, Andy. 1984. "Owens Ran Cinder Track." Jesse Owens Museum (16 August). Available at: http://www.jesseowensmuseum.org/index.cfm?fuseaction=res_viewDetails&id=34. Accessed October 9, 2006.

Author. 2007. "Title of Article." *Runner's World* (42) 3: 74.

Schwartz, Larry. "Owens Pierced a Myth." ESPN. Available at: http://espn. go.com/sportscentury/features/00016393.html. Accessed December 30, 2006.

Sheehan, Joseph M. 1935. "Owens's Record-breaking Feats Presage Brilliant Olympic Mark." *New York Times* (2 June): S2.

Shulman, Steven. 2004. *The Impact of Immigration on African Americans.* New Brunswick, N.J.: Transaction Publishers.

Streissguth, Thomas. 2006. *Jesse Owens.* Sports Heroes and Legends. Minneapolis, Minn.: Lerner Publications.

Tyack, David. 2003. *Seeking Common Ground: Public Schools in a Diverse Society.* Cambridge, Mass.: Harvard University Press.

United States Holocaust Memorial Museum. "Nazification of Sport." Available at http://www.ushmm.org/museum/exhibit/online/Olympics/ zcb013.htm. Accessed December 10, 2006.

Wallace, Wendy. 1986. "Tracking a Legend." Jesse Owens Museum (1 May). Available at: http://www.jesseowensmuseum.org/index. cfm?fuseaction=res_viewDetails&id=35. Accessed October 9, 2006.

The Wonderful, Horrible Life of Leni Riefenstahl. 1993. New York: Kino Video, 2003. DVD.

Young, A. S. Doc. 1970. " 'My Name Has Never Been Tom'; Blackthink Blackthink." Review of *Blackthink*, by Jesse Owens. *New York Times* (3 May): 278.

Zinn, Howard. 2003. *A People's History of the United States: 1492–Present.* New York: HarperCollins.

INDEX

About the Author

JACQUELINE EDMONDSON is Associate Dean for Teacher Education and Undergraduate Programs at Pennsylvania State University. She is the author of *Condoleezza Rice: A Biography* (Greenwood, 2006) and *Venus and Serena Williams: A Biography* (Greenwood, 2005).

CPSIA information can be obtained at www.ICGtesting.com
Printed in the USA
BVOW03*1403011014

368971BV00007B/113/P

9 780313 339882